FACE IT AND FIX IT

FACE IT
AND
FIX IT

A Three-Step Plan
to Break Free
from Denial and Discover
the Life You Deserve

Ken Seeley with Myatt Murphy

HarperOne
An Imprint of HarperCollinsPublishers

HarperOne

HarperCollins books may be purchased for educational, business, or sales promotional use. For information please write: Special Markets Department, HarperCollins Publishers, 10 East 53rd Street, New York, NY 10022.

HarperCollins Web site: http://www.harpercollins.com
HarperCollins®, 📖 ®, and HarperOne™ are
trademarks of HarperCollins Publishers

FIRST EDITION
Designed by Level C

Library of Congress Cataloging-in-Publication Data
Seeley, Ken.
Face it & fix it : a three step plan to break free from denial and discover the life
you deserve / by Ken Seeley. — 1st ed.
p. cm.
ISBN 978–0–06–169698–5
1. Denial (Psychology)   2. Defense mechanisms (Psychology)   3. Self-deception.
4. Self-defeating behavior.   I. Title.   II. Title: Face it and fix it.
BF175.5.D44S44   2009
158.1—dc22   2009004880

09 10 11 12 13 RRD (H) 10 9 8 7 6 5 4 3 2 1

To my parents,
Ray and Naomi Seeley,
and to all those who are suffering in emotional pain.
I hope this gives you relief.

Contents

Part 3
Turning Denial into Balance

Introduction

Right now, you could be hiding something from yourself. Something that's holding you back, whether physically, financially, socially, or spiritually.

Don't worry . . . you're not alone.

We are all in denial about something. It might be an issue or behavior that's small and seemingly innocent, such as accepting that you're not trying to excel in your job as much as you could be. Or it might be an issue or behavior that's much larger and potentially lethal, such as a full-blown addiction that, at this very moment, could be destroying your life and/or the lives of those you love. The truth is that, no matter who you are, and no matter how insignificant or overwhelming your problems may seem, something is holding you back from living your life to the fullest. How do I know this?

Because I've spent nearly half my life in denial, and it almost killed me more times than I can count.

Maybe, like most people who know me, you're familiar with *Intervention,* the TV show on A&E where I'm blessed to step into the lives of families who desperately need help conquering some of the world's most severe addictions. What many don't know is that before I began helping others, I was someone who desperately needed help myself, not just with the addictions I would eventually fall into but also with the denial that kept me from seeing how these addictions were damaging my life.

You see, up until the age of fifteen, I never felt comfortable in my own skin. Nothing in me ever felt good—until the day I first tried alcohol. With that first drink, I suddenly felt an immediate connection: I had finally found a tool that seemed to bring me the sense of comfort I was seeking. Thanks to a few fake IDs, I became a regular at the local bars at age sixteen. But as peaceful as alcohol made me feel, it made me wonder what else might have the same effect in filling the void I felt inside. That's when my addiction to alcohol shifted toward drugs.

The drinking led to taking pick-me-up pills called black beauties. From the black beauties, I quickly moved on to taking mescaline, a hallucinogenic recreational drug. Chasing a new high from the mescaline, I began dropping acid. With each new drug I tried, I became happier with who I was. I didn't think I was causing damage to myself, because I finally felt great. I didn't think I was hurting anyone else, because I was finally accepted by my peers, even though they were also drug abusers. I just seemed to be more connected with the world—I finally felt good about being Ken. That was because denial had already clouded my thoughts and kept me from seeing my destructive behaviors for what they really were.

By the time I left for the Air Force at eighteen to escape the scrutiny of my parents, I was a full-blown drug addict. My parents prayed that military discipline would put a stop to my bad habits, but it only made them flourish. Alcohol was acceptable in the armed forces, and after training I was transferred to Italy, where my problems only got worse. I began smoking hashish, the most potent form of marijuana there is, and then had acid and mescaline sent over from the United States. When my apartment was raided, my drug addiction got me thrown out of the Air Force.

You would think that having my military career crumble would wake me up to the seriousness of my actions, yet my denial was so strong that I still couldn't connect the dots. Because my denial had me believing that my family wanted to control me when all they really wanted was for me to get better, I moved away from them. That was when my addictions really took off.

I celebrated my twenty-first birthday in a blackout on cocaine. I started experimenting with even more dangerous drugs, including ecstasy and crystal meth. I moved to California, as far away from my family as possible, and showed up for holidays only if I was sober enough to get to the airport. Being too hungover or too high to work caused me to lose every job I held. Yet through it all, one thing never changed: I stayed in denial about what was interfering with my life, until the day someone made me face what I was ignoring head-on.

In my midtwenties, I found a waitering job from a man who owned not only his own restaurant but his own treatment center for addicts. A recovering addict himself, he believed in me more than I believed in myself at that time. His faith in me was so strong that I quickly went from being a waiter to managing his restaurant, then handling his accounting, then eventually doing the medical billing at his treatment center. I never believed I could do any of the things he asked me to do, yet his constant faith in my abilities kept me grounded and in control. Until the day he finally sat me down to discuss what I had been in denial about for twelve years—my addictions.

He brought in his director (the person who taught him how to run an intervention) and sat me down, along with all of my co-workers. They told me they loved me, but they refused to love me to death and basically told me to "get help or good luck, because you're not working here anymore until you make the right choice." People believe that addicts need to be ready to flip that switch and make a change in their life, but that's not true. I was nowhere near ready to want that change. People would tell me all the time that I needed help. Even some of the people I partied with felt that I was over the edge and needed to stop. But the denial was so overwhelming that I would never allow myself to see what my life had become. I wasn't ready to change, but they created an environment that forced me to take the first step, so I figured I'd try this thirty-day treatment thing everyone told me I should try.

That's where the miracle happened: my wall of denial finally came down. Through treatment, I got the education I needed to realize that all of the failures in my life were related to my addictions. I finally saw that denial had kept me from seeing the truth—that what I thought was making me happy was actually keeping me from being happy in the first place.

Without denial in my life, I could finally connect the dots. I realized that my behaviors were behind every job loss I had experienced. I realized that my behaviors were behind being thrown out of the military and missing out on a possible career in the armed forces. I realized that my behaviors had closed off my life and made me isolated, keeping anyone and anything from ever getting through. But most important, I realized that my behaviors were going to kill me and that if I didn't do something about them, I was months—maybe weeks—away from dying. Over the years I had watched people I partied with, many of whom were less addicted than I was, overdose and die. I knew what I was doing could be fatal, yet denial always kept me from believing that one day I would be the next casualty. Once the denial was lifted, I was able to own my actions and behaviors and finally take the necessary steps toward correcting them.

It has been twenty years since my last drink- or drug-induced high, and I've never felt so fulfilled in every facet of my life—personally, professionally, emotionally, and spiritually. But I'm reminded of the hold that denial can have over a life each and every day I go to work. My clients, who range from those eking out a meager existence to multimillionaires, need my professional assistance to help them handle a wide assortment of life-threatening addictions, including alcoholism, drug dependency, excessive gambling, sexual compulsion, abusive behaviors, and mental disorders, just to name a few. The people I've helped and the problems they have faced may have been of many different kinds, but they all have something in common: denial.

Denial is the number one symptom, not just of all addictions, but also of nearly every other disorder, behavior, or habit that may be affecting your life negatively. Have you been finding yourself falling behind every once in a while with your bills, your studies, or your work, yet you can't seem to figure out why? Have you been watching friends slip out of your life and finding it hard to bring them back in, or wondering why you have so much trouble attracting new friends? Have you felt that something is missing from your life, yet you just can't understand why the things you want always seem to be out of your reach? You could have a problem that's causing you to ask these questions—and affecting not just you but those around you— but denial is preventing you from ever being aware that anything is wrong.

Until now, that is.

This book is your guide to understanding the true nature of denial and the ways in which it prevents you from being complete. With this book, you'll not only be able to recognize whether you—or those around you—are in denial, but you'll also learn the tools I use with some of my toughest clients to put an end once and for all to denial and the hidden problems that cause it, no matter how severe or insignificant they may be. You can turn to this book at any point in your life when you suspect that denial is affecting you—right now, five months from now, or five years down the road—and use it to instantly spot and stop denial and the behaviors it hides.

To be blunt, it's a book I wish I had read when I was fifteen, before I ever took that first drink.

For me, denial covered up a series of addictions that poisoned my life. For you, denial may be doing the same, or it may be hiding some less severe behavior that nevertheless is throwing your life out of balance and preventing you from being as happy, healthy, and fulfilled as you could be. Let me show you how to see what denial may be hiding from you, so that you can finally have the perfect life you deserve.

> Ken Seeley, BRI II, CNDAI, RASi
> Founder of Intervention911, board-
> registered interventionist II, and
> A&E interventionist

Part 1

The Power of Denial

1

The Definition of Denial

Before you begin reading this book, I want you to answer ten easy yes-or-no questions. Don't think too hard about them, and don't dwell on examples or incidents that might make you give one answer over the other. Don't give an answer that's in between yes and no, such as maybe, sometimes, or it depends. Instead, simply write down—on a separate piece of paper, not in this book—the first answer that comes into your head, either yes or no.

1. Do you often feel depressed, angry, or anxious for no reason?

2. Have any of your friends, family members, co-workers, or anyone else close to you shown any concern about you recently—even if for no reason at all?

3. Do you spend a lot of your time judging other people?

4. Are you falling behind in any important areas of your life—work, family time, personal life?

5. Do you find yourself avoiding some situations (events, parties, special occasions) because certain people will be present?

6. Do you find yourself wanting and needing to be the center of attention?

7. Do you feel your life will get better or easier if a specific thing happens?

8. Do you tend to sweat the small stuff?

9. Do you constantly second-guess yourself after making decisions?

10. Have you noticed a decline in your health or appearance?

Now that you have your answers, make sure they are honestly from your heart. Did you answer these questions truthfully and quickly without putting too much thought into them? If you didn't, then I want you to answer them again, because your answers to these questions are the key to getting the most out of this book. These ten simple answers will be what finally helps you achieve the happy, successful life you've always dreamed about but have never been able to accomplish . . . until now, that is.

THE DEFINITION OF DENIAL

So what exactly is denial?

One of our most primitive defensive reactions, denial is an unconscious and natural coping mechanism that allows us to refuse to identify or acknowledge the existence or significance of unpleasant external circumstances or internal feelings and thoughts. By allowing us to ignore distressing situations and essentially distort how we see reality, denial is a psychological survival strategy that our brains set in motion in order to give us time to adapt to and heal from a wide assortment of threatening conditions, such as pain, stress, anxiety, and traumatic feelings or events.

If that long explanation sounds a bit confusing, I have another definition that may be a little easier to grasp. Simply put: denial keeps us blind to the things we don't want to see because our minds don't feel we're ready to handle them.

A little bit of denial in your life can actually be beneficial, but it's an unconscious reaction that has a way of growing or sticking around a lot longer than it needs to. When left unchecked, denial can be incredibly toxic if it prevents you from dealing with problems or issues that demand immediate action or change, especially when those problems or issues are affecting your life in an unhealthy way. For instance, if you have some bad habits, a personality disorder, a life-threatening addiction, or a health problem that needs to be treated, a little bit of denial can go a long way in creating a much bigger dilemma. That's when denial's repercussions can affect every aspect of your life in a negative, harmful way.

ARE YOU IN DENIAL? THE ANSWER IS YES!

As an interventionist, I've helped hundreds of addicts break free of some of the worst cases of denial I've ever seen. For nearly each and every addict I've worked with over the years, the layers of denial were so thick that they might have seemed impossible to shatter. But after eight years and close to one thousand interventions, I've come to understand something fundamental about denial: we are all in denial about something.

Maybe you're not in denial about being a full-blown alcoholic. Maybe you're not in denial about having an eating disorder, a drug problem, or a sex addiction that could be placing your life at serious risk. And because you're not in denial about any of these things, maybe you think this book couldn't possibly be helpful to you. But that's where you would be wrong.

No matter who we are—regardless of our background, education, financial status, race, nationality, and sex—we are all not just susceptible to denial but actually in some form of denial at all times. The mistake most people make is in thinking that denial is lying in wait until some major catastrophe shakes it loose and forces it to take control. In actuality, denial is always present. It operates 24/7 in all of us on some conscious or unconscious level, blurring or blocking our perception about the behaviors, actions, thoughts, events, and emotions in our lives that are hazardous.

For my uncle, it was something as simple as not seeing a doctor to address some medical issues he was dealing with. For years, he had problems swallowing his food and breathing on occasion. Everyone could see there was something wrong—everyone except him. Whenever he was asked about his health, he just denied his difficulties and treated them as annoyances instead of the major problems we all knew them to be.

When he retired, he finally went to a doctor, not for help with the chronic issues he had ignored for almost a decade but for a routine physical. That's when he was diagnosed with stage 4 cancer. The cancer had spread throughout his entire body and most of his organs. My uncle lived only a few months after that. If he had addressed the physical problems he was having instead of denying them, he could have been treated in time. Denial kept him from getting the help he needed and enjoying the many years he had in front of him.

What you are in denial about may seem insignificant to you. It might be a quirky habit, or a character trait you think of as an asset instead of a flaw. What you're in denial about can range from the trivial to the traumatic. But you *are* in denial—at this very moment—about something. And no matter how unimportant that something may seem, sustaining your denial about it is detracting from other areas of your life that may be withering away.

Right now, denial is at the heart of something negative happening to you, if not several negative things happening to you at once. If you've ever felt that your life isn't running as perfectly as you always thought it would, denial may be to blame. If you've ever felt held back, treated unfairly, discriminated against, or passed up, denial could be at the heart of that feeling. If you've ever felt lost, depressed, ashamed, embarrassed, nervous, scared, or angry, denial may be the reason. Most important, if you feel that something is missing from your life but you just can't put a finger on what it is, then it isn't that you're probably in denial—you're definitely in denial.

CAN YOU ESCAPE DENIAL? THE ANSWER IS YES!

What makes denial difficult is that it leaves you clueless that you're unconsciously letting something unhealthy into your life. But what can make it deadly is that it prevents you from getting the help you need—or allowing those who love you to help you.

- I've known people whose character traits kept them from moving forward in their career, having a stable relationship, staying on top of their finances, or just feeling happier more often.

- I've spoken to people who were suffering from a persistent fear, physical problem, or mental disorder that prevented them from participating in certain life-enriching activities, kept them from being around people who would have been healthy for their spirit, and even placed them—or their loved ones—at risk.

- I've worked with people with habits and behaviors that slowly drained away portions of their life they thought they would never get back—financial, physical, emotional, psychological, or all of the above.

- I've known people with problems that weren't their fault but that affected them daily because they refused to break free and escape from them.

It doesn't matter how much happiness denial has caused you to miss out on. It doesn't even matter how much damage denial has done to your life. It doesn't matter how many important occasions, business opportunities, loving relationships, esteem-boosting experiences, and life-changing moments you haven't had. Yes, you are in denial about something, but no, you're not stuck in denial forever. Or, I should say, you don't have to be stuck in denial forever. No matter how deep or how far you have sunk into your denial, there is always a way out—if you know how to break it down and keep it down for good.

THE WALL OF DENIAL

When I describe denial to the families I work with during my interventions, I ask them to picture a brick wall.

Denial is something your mind builds all around you, brick by brick, so that it blocks your view from all sides. Every time you turn a blind eye to a problem—whether one of your own or someone else's—you're laying down a brick. Every time you lie to cover up your actions or those of someone you care about, you're laying down a brick. Every single time you say something, do something, or think something that dismisses, denies, or ignores a problem or issue that's negatively affecting you or someone you love, you're laying down a brick.

Denial is a process that keeps going and going and going until all you're left with is a seemingly impenetrable wall you can't see over or get around. This wall completely shields you from the helpful opinions of others, the consequences of your own actions, and the reality of your situation. It's a wall built on ignoring the truth about certain unhealthy aspects of your life or the actions of others. This wall stands between you and what will make you feel healthier, happier, and more fulfilled.

So how does anyone break through the wall?

When families are desperate to save a loved one from a hard-core addiction, they call someone like me, a trained interventionist who breaks down the wall of denial and shows them how to keep it down for good. I truly hope your problem is not that serious, but whatever you're in denial of, it has still built a wall that surrounds you.

Something needs to intervene. Something needs to happen in your life that will not just show you what you're in denial about, but also make you uncomfortable enough to finally do something to end it. That's when the wall starts to crack and finally fall down. Sometimes it can be something as simple as noticing that the details of your life are changing too quickly. For one client of mine, it was shopping for new, bigger, clothes three times in a matter of months, then falling into debt just to pay for it all; it took his shrinking finances to help him realize he was in denial of having a weight problem. For you, however, it may not be that simple.

The individuals I've educated over the past eight years have been some of the most severe deniers you'll ever meet. In that time, I've discovered that deniers can be divided into two groups: those who succumb to their wall, and those who succeed in tearing it down. Those who succumb always take a halfhearted approach. For some, the wall may come down temporarily, but the minute they start feeling good about themselves again or their lives improve, they begin to build the wall right back up by succumbing to their old ways. Or they may try to break their wall down slowly, brick by brick, using the least amount of effort possible. They may curb their behaviors slightly—for instance, by not doing them on certain days—but this approach is like throwing a firecracker at the wall and believing that one tiny explosion will take it down.

Those who succeed do things a bit differently. The deniers I've helped turn their lives around didn't reach for firecrackers to knock down their wall. Instead, they tossed bombs at their wall by making immediate and significant changes in their lives. They made decisions that left no part of their wall standing—and they stuck with those decisions. Then they put the right steps in motion—and called on the right people for support—to bring in a bulldozer to wipe out any part of their wall that was left over, so that it would never rebuild itself.

No matter what may be holding you back that denial doesn't want you to see, you're about to join those who succeed. The purpose of this book is to help you recognize denial, build your bomb, break through your wall, and bring your bulldozer in to ensure that your wall never gets built up again. Whether the denial is in your own life or in the life of someone you care about, this book will be many things for you: it will be your bomb as well as your bulldozer, and it will break down your wall of denial so that you can finally see and experience what's been waiting for you behind it.

A happy fulfilled life.

Now put your bricks down and let's get started together.

2

The Things We Deny
the Most

Right now I'm not sure exactly what you're in denial about, and chances are that you have no idea either—yet! But until we figure that out together, using the tools in this book, I can say with absolute assurance that whatever is preventing you from having the best life possible falls into at least one of the following categories:

- Abuse

- Disorders (psychological or emotional)

- Addiction

- Physical (health) issues

- (The) Truth, about both ourselves and those around us

These five areas are the places where denial most frequently tries to cloud our awareness so that it can protect us from our own reality. Together they form the acronym ADAPT, and for good reason: in all five areas, our minds use denial to adapt to painful or difficult situations.

But it's not an adaptation that helps you grow. Instead, denial just makes it easier for you to drive around your problems instead of removing them. The real issue in your life—which is somewhere in the following five lists—is still sitting there in the middle of the road, causing a mini–traffic jam that's keeping your life from moving forward.

Personally, I never felt like I was a part of anything when I was growing up. From grade school through high school, I just never seemed to fit in with the rest of the kids. I never understood why, but it felt at the time like a situation I could never change. When I began using alcohol as an escape, a part of me knew it was wrong to do that, but denial stepped in to blind me to the problems alcohol was causing in my life. Denial made it that much easier to blame those around me instead of facing things head-on.

When you let denial happen—instead of trying to find it and remove it so you can face your problems head-on and beat them—you're choosing to live in a darkness that's actually changeable. You're robbing yourself of your true potential for happiness and preventing yourself from getting from point A to point B.

Point A is where you're at now.

Point B is the better life you deserve.

You and I are about to go from point A to point B together. But for now, let me explain the five areas where denial loves to grow, which I call the ADAPT list.

ABUSE

Denial and abuse go hand in hand. Denial can blur the perception of the person who is abusive, the perception of the person who is being abused, or the perception of both individuals at the same time. For the abuser, staying in denial keeps his or her behaviors from being judged or punished. The abused ones may opt to remain in denial rather than admit that someone—especially a person they love dearly—is capable of hurting them or someone else, physically, emotionally, or financially.

The most common forms of abuse are

- *Child abuse:* Over 3 million incidents are reported each year, although experts suspect that number may be three times larger.

- *Domestic violence (also known as spousal abuse):* This type of abuse is the most common form of injury of women between the ages of fifteen and forty-four. In the U.S., approximately 1.3 million women and 835,000 men are physically assaulted by their partner every year.

- *Elder abuse:* According to statistics, 1 million to 2 million Americans over sixty-five have been hurt, exploited, or mistreated by someone they depend on for care and protection.

- *Financial/economic abuse:* It's estimated that one out of every twenty-five senior citizens is the victim of economic abuse, or roughly 5 million every year.

- *Pet abuse:* Animal abuse is not just illegal in all fifty states but an indicator of a much greater threat. The National Coalition Against Domestic Violence found that 85 percent of women and 63 percent of children who had been victims of domestic violence reported incidents of pet abuse by their abuser.

- *Parental alienation syndrome:* This psychological condition—typically seen in children whose parents are involved in a divorce or separation—is the mental manipulation of children by one parent that can ruin the relationship the children share with the other parent.

- *Sexual abuse:* One in six women and one in thirty-three men will be sexually assaulted or molested in their lifetime.

DISORDERS (PSYCHOLOGICAL OR EMOTIONAL)

HBO shows like *The Sopranos* and *In Treatment* may make the idea of visiting a doctor or therapist more acceptable, but most people still feel embarrassed to admit that they may have a problem with their brain. That embarrassment is the fuel for denial, preventing many deniers from ever seeking help for conditions that might easily be curable. When you realize that one out of every four American adults suffers from a diagnosable mental disorder each year, you can see how this problem is much more common than you would imagine.

The most common types of mental issues and disorders include

- *Specific phobia:* About 19.2 million American adults suffer from some type of specific phobia (a constant fear and avoidance of a specific thing or situation).

- *Body dysmorphia (BDD):* Research suggests that 1 to 2 percent of the U.S. population is obsessed with either an imagined or perceived minor defect in their appearance.

- *Autism:* About one out of every 150 children born in the United States suffers from autism—or between 1 million and 1.5 million children.

- *Schizophrenia, delusion, or dementia:* About 2.4 million American adults (close to 1.1 percent of the population) over the age of eighteen suffer from schizophrenia.

- *Antisocial personality:* This condition is characterized by chronic behavior that violates others without guilt or remorse and is found in an estimated 7.6 million Americans.

- *Attention deficit hyperactivity disorder (ADD, ADHD):* ADHD is the most commonly diagnosed neurobehavioral disorder in children. It's also estimated that between 4 and 6 percent of adults continue to deal with ADHD.

- *Post-traumatic stress disorder (PTSD):* About 8 percent of the U.S. population will have PTSD symptoms at some point in their lives—it's estimated that over 5 million adults experience PTSD every year.

- *Borderline personality:* About 2 percent of adults suffer from this disorder that impairs the emotions and causes excessive impulsive behavior.

- *Seasonal affective disorder (SAD):* This form of depression is triggered by the change of seasons and affects 10 million Americans a year.

- *Dependent personality/separation anxiety:* Being overly dependent on others to the point of feeling angst-ridden when they're away afflicts roughly 7 percent of Americans at some point in their lives.

- *Obsessive-compulsive disorders (OCD):* One of every fifty U.S. adults engages in some form of OCD behavior, such as hoarding, kleptomania, or mysophobia (fear of germs).

- *Dysthymia:* Dysthymia is minor depression that affects 3.3 million American adults each year. The median age of onset is thirty-one.

- *Major depressive disorder:* Affecting approximately 14.8 million adults, a major depressive disorder is the leading cause of disability in the United States for people between the ages of fifteen and forty-four.

- *Bipolar disorder:* Bipolar disorders include bipolar 1, bipolar 2, and cyclothymia. The National Institute of Mental Health believes that bipolar disorder affects more than 2.5 million adult Americans every year.

- *Postpartum depression:* One in eight women who give birth suffer from postpartum mood disorders, yet only 20 percent ever bother to seek help for it.

- *Panic attacks:* According to the National Institute of Mental Health, over 3 million Americans will experience a panic disorder sometime in their lives.

- *Oppositional defiant disorder:* This disorder is characterized by a constant pattern of arguing, throwing tantrums, being angry, or engaging in disruptive behaviors toward authority figures. According to the Mayo Clinic, as many as one in ten children may have ODD during their childhood.

- *Paranoid disorder:* Paranoid disorder is any condition that leads to feelings of genuine mistrust of others.

ADDICTION

According to the National Center on Addiction and Substance Abuse, one out of every four Americans will have a drug- or alcohol-related problem in their lifetime. That's over 75 million people in the United States alone. In addition, there are other forms of addiction that may not be as lethal but can certainly harm your health and well-being when you cover them up with denial.

The most common addictions are

- *Alcoholism:* Over 14 million Americans deal with this form of addiction.

- *Substance abuse:* Although the United States is home to only 4 percent of the world's population, its citizens use 66 percent of the world's illegal drugs.

- *Food addiction/ eating disorders:* Eating disorders include bulimia nervosa, anorexia nervosa, and binge eating. Over 10 million females and 1 million males struggle with anorexia or bulimia.

- *Problem gambling:* Between 4 million and 6 million U.S. adults are considered to be problem gamblers, with an additional 2 million estimated to be pathological gamblers.

- *Sexual compulsion:* It's estimated that between 3 and 5 percent of Americans meet the criteria for sexual addiction and compulsivity.

- *Nicotine addiction:* This addiction affects over 60 million Americans.

- *Computer addiction (or Internet addiction disorder):* It's estimated that 15 million to 30 million Americans suffer from this fairly new condition.

- *Work addiction:* According to a recent study from the University of California, Santa Barbara, at least 31 percent of college-educated male workers admit that they work more than fifty hours per week.

- *Caffeine addiction:* Caffeine is the most commonly used psycho-active drug in the world—over 170 million people are hooked in the United States alone.

- *Video game addiction:* A 2007 Harris poll discovered that 8.5 percent of young gamers (ages eight to eighteen) in the United States can be classified as clinically addicted to video games.

PHYSICAL (HEALTH) ISSUES

You might think that denial would be impossible when the issues it's trying to mask are physical. Whether the problem is a chronic illness, the natural erosion that comes with getting older, or simply an unexplained itch, ache, or pain, denial is still a defense that can distort reality enough to prevent you from learning the uncomfortable truth about what could be happening to your health, body, or appearance.

The most common physical problems and health issues include

- *Loss of memory/mild cognitive impairment:* Cognitive problems can be caused by degenerative diseases such as Alzheimer's, which currently afflicts over 5 million Americans, according to the Centers for Disease Control (CDC), which estimates that this number may rise as high as 16 million by 2030.

- *Being overweight/obese:* As of 2009, 34 percent of Americans are obese and 32.7 percent are overweight.

- *Hair loss:* Hereditary hair loss affects approximately 50 million American men and 30 million American women.

- *Eye and vision problems:* The Vision Council of America states that more than 11 million Americans have an uncorrected visual impairment that is affecting their quality of life.

- *Communication disorder:* This kind of disorder includes deafness, balance disorders, and speech problems. It's estimated that over 46 million Americans deal with some type of disordered communication.

- *Loss of mobility or motor skills:* Old age or a wide variety of diseases and conditions can affect a person's motor skills.

- *Dermatological problems:* Skin problems include skin cancer, actinic keratoses, rosacea, eczema, and psoriasis. Experts say that one in five Americans will develop skin cancer in their lifetime.

- *High blood pressure (hypertension):* It's estimated that one out of four American adults are affected by this life-threatening health condition.

- *Cancer:* According to the American Cancer Society, it was expected that 1,437,180 new cancer cases would be diagnosed in 2008 alone.

- *Diabetes:* The CDC estimates that, although more than 20.8 million Americans have diabetes, 6.2 million aren't aware that they have the disease.

- *Allergies:* Allergic disease is the fifth-leading chronic disease in the United States.

- *Chronic fatigue syndrome (CFS):* CFS affects more Americans than multiple sclerosis, lupus, lung cancer, or ovarian cancer. According to the CDC, more than 1 million Americans have CFS.

- *Sexually transmitted infections (STI):* According to the American Social Health Association, more than half of all people will have an STI at some point in their lives.

- *Poor hygiene:* Hygiene issues include conditions such as body odor and halitosis, a bacterial condition that affects more than 60 percent of all Americans.

- *Birth defects or developmental disabilities:* One of thirty-three babies is born with a birth defect.

(THE) TRUTH

Finally, most people assume that denial is a response to serious matters that have nothing to do with them. Depending on your age, your health, your personal habits, and your history, you may not have identified with any of the issues I've just listed. That could make it much harder to believe that there is something about which even you are in denial.

Denial can hide any of the myriad issues, behaviors, feelings, and attitudes that all of us have a problem with at one time or another. It's how you choose to handle each of these problems when it enters your life that shows whether you rely on denial to hide your problems or whether you are comfortable in addressing them. If you accept the truth when it comes at you, it's much easier for you to address it—or even embrace it. But if you doubt the truth when it's presented to you, then even if you're an otherwise well-balanced person, you can quickly and unexpectedly find yourself using denial to cover up the facts.

The most common negative situations, emotions, and personality traits are

- *Arrogance:* Being overbearing or dominating.

- *Codependence:* Compulsively trying to take care of someone else who has problems or issues cited on the ADAPT list.

- *Excessive infatuation:* Feeling an attraction to someone who isn't aware of your feelings. According to the Stalking Resource Center, one in twelve women and one in forty-five men will be stalked in their lifetime, and 1,006,970 women and 370,990 men are stalked in the United States annually.

- *Financial irresponsibility or debt:* Two-thirds of Americans aren't saving enough for retirement, and the average household owes a total of over $8,500.

- *Greed:* Being gluttonous or stingy.

- *Ignorance:* Overlooking or ignoring the fact that someone you care about suffers from a problem or issue on the ADAPT list.

- *Inferiority:* Feeling stupid or substandard around others.

- *Infidelity:* Either your own or that of your partner.

- *Jealousy:* Being envious of others.

- *Lack of accountability:* Staying oblivious to an upcoming job or duty, such as parenthood or supporting someone in need.

- *Lack of passion:* Falling out of love with someone or something.

- *Maliciousness:* Being spiteful and mean toward others.

- *Narcissism:* Being obsessed with yourself.

- *Nonacceptance:* Refusing to accept the death of a loved one.

- *Prejudice:* Being racist, judgmental, or disapproving toward others based on factors that have nothing to do with their actual character.

- *Procrastination:* Being unmotivated or lazy.

- *Rejection:* Refusing to accept that you're not the right person for a specific task, position, or duty.

- *Repressed sexuality:* Having feelings for the same sex, but not being able to express them.

- *Stubbornness:* Being wrong or inflexible.

- *Trust issues:* Being afraid of commitment or intimacy.

3

Balance and Denial: Why You Can't Have Both

No matter how much you believe it's not true, everyone has some type of denial going on in their life. Denial ranges from covering up something so insignificant that it doesn't seem to affect one's life in a major way to shrouding an immense and potentially toxic secret. Wherever it falls on this spectrum, denial is there in our lives, and I have a simple way to help my clients understand this idea.

Imagine that your life is faultless in every possible way. Picture yourself getting everything you need physically, spiritually, and emotionally, not just from those around you but from within. All of your needs are completely satisfied, every dream and goal you've ever had for yourself is instantly realized, and every possible problem you might encounter is easily resolved the moment it appears. If you ever were to have this type of existence, it would mean one thing: your life would be in perfect balance.

When your life is in perfect balance, it's impossible to be in denial because being in denial would mean you're consciously or unconsciously refusing to admit the existence of a problem in your life. If you were actually lucky enough to have a problem-free life—a life in perfect balance—you wouldn't have anything to deny. Is that your life? Then let me ask you a few questions:

- Is your life all happiness and no stress?

- Are you completely free of negative emotions such as depression, anxiety, anger, and loneliness?

- Is your self-esteem always at an all-time high?

- Would you consider yourself successful as a person—meaning not with your job or career but with how you and others perceive the real you?

Are you finding it hard to see yourself in this perfect state of being, where life gives you everything you need and fixes every problem at its source? Can you honestly say that your life is in perfect balance? Of course not. The truth is that no one's life is ever in perfect balance. And if it takes a perfectly balanced life to be free of denial, and yours is far from that, can you see why there's no question in my mind—and shouldn't be in yours—that you're in denial about something?

Maybe it's not your entire life that's out of balance, but only some part of it. It doesn't have to be something catastrophic that's pulling you out of balance. You may seem to have a perfect life in one area—such as with your family life, your work, your physical health, or your finances—but achieving perfection in this one area could be putting a strain on other areas. The fact is that each of us has something, if not many things, in our lives that could easily be improved—if we learn how to find them and focus on them.

When your life is in perfect balance, you divide your day up in such a way that you spend every minute doing things that are healthy for your body, mind, and spirit. That means doing things that bring you genuine feelings of comfort, satisfaction, and happiness, such as enjoying time with family and friends, striving toward—or staying on top of—all of your life goals, or actively pursuing your dreams.

When your life is out of balance, you spend far less time doing the things that are healthy for your body, mind, and spirit and far more time doing things that instead are unhealthy, such as turning to an addiction, developing a disorder, or feeling negative emotions such as anger and jealousy. There are two possible reasons for the imbalance that comes from doing things that are counterproductive to having a full and complete life:

1. *You don't have enough healthy things to turn to in your life.* Maybe you lack for friends and others who care about you. Maybe you don't have many goals, or the ones you do have seem unattainable to you. Perhaps you gave up on your dreams a long time ago. Regardless of the reasons, deniers who don't have as many healthy options in their life tend to reach for an unhealthy action, behavior, habit, or activity—if not several—to fill the void inside. In their mind, these unhealthy alternatives work, but all they've done is create a false sense of balance.

The problem is that the more unhealthy behaviors and activities you have in your life, the more likely it is that the few healthy elements you may have in your life will suffer or disappear. And the more that happens, the more susceptible you become to filling the resulting holes in your life with new unhealthy things. It's a vicious cycle that causes your denial to grow by stacking more and more bricks onto your wall of denial.

2. *The unhealthy things in your life may be stealing away the time you would spend on healthier things.* Many unhealthy actions, behaviors, and activities are habit-forming. Because denial has a way of making you believe you aren't doing anything unhealthy, each and every minute you spend doing something negative means another minute not spent doing something positive. This creates the same vicious cycle—everything healthy in your life begins to shrink while everything unhealthy in your life continues to grow.

AN IMBALANCED LIFE EQUALS A LIB

With so many negative things out there capable of tilting your life off-balance, you might think it would be next to impossible to offer advice about every possible problem. That's where you would be wrong. No matter what you're doing now that's keeping you from staying balanced, no matter what you may be suffering from, no matter how inconsequential or extreme your situation may be, every single negative thing that can cause your life to shift out of balance falls under one heading: they are all what I refer to as "life-imbalancing behaviors," or LIB for short.

In a nutshell, a LIB is any negative behavior that prevents you from doing something positive instead.

1. A LIB can be an unhealthy habit, such as biting your nails, suffering from trust issues, or procrastinating too much.

2. A LIB can be an unhealthy trait, such as being stubborn, malicious, prejudiced, or arrogant.

3. A LIB can be an unhealthy behavior, such as being financially irresponsible, being unaccountable, cheating on your partner, denying your true sexuality, or being codependent.

4. A LIB can be an unhealthy emotion, such as feeling inferior or rejected, being obsessed with someone, or losing desire for someone you should desire.

5. A LIB can be an unhealthy desire, such as greed or jealousy.

6. Finally, a LIB can be simply ignoring an unhealthy problem that's affecting your life or the life of someone close to you, such as closing your eyes to a physical or mental health issue, having an addiction, being abused, or any of the above.

THINK OF YOUR LIB AS THE PIECE
THAT DOESN'T REALLY FIT

If you imagine a life in balance as a puzzle that has all the pieces in place, a life out of balance is one that's missing certain pieces. Instead of filling those holes by looking for and finding the right pieces in ourselves, we use a LIB as a temporary piece so that our puzzle will at least seem complete. But a LIB never fits, and worse yet, it causes other pieces, such as friends, family, stability, and self-esteem, to shake loose.

By using your LIB as a replacement piece in your life, you risk losing other valuable pieces that you may never get back. The more pieces you lose, the more tempting it becomes to use other LIBs to fill all the new holes in your puzzle caused by your first LIB. Using LIBs this way eventually becomes an endless cycle that causes you to rely on them even more as time passes.

So why on earth would any of us want to ruin our lives doing something negative when we could choose to do something positive instead? The reasons we turn to LIBs can vary.

For most people, a LIB fills an emotional need for something they feel they are lacking in their life, such as a stronger sense of self-esteem, comfort, security, happiness, or a calmer state of mind. For others, a LIB may offer relief from feeling pain or emptiness within. Still others may turn to a LIB because it's the only thing that makes them feel safe or comfortable in their own skin. Regardless of the reason, we all turn to some type of LIB to replace whatever may be missing from our lives.

That's why LIBs are so infectious and difficult to remove from our lives, and why denial likes to hide them from us—so we can't find them and remove them. As unhealthy as a LIB may be, for most deniers it can feel like the only thing keeping their life together, even though it's often the main reason their life may be falling apart.

What's ironic is that the word *lib* means "liberation," which is exactly the opposite of what a LIB does in your life. A life-imbalancing behavior can change how you spend your day, from the moment you wake up until the moment you go to bed. And in some cases it can even affect how much sleep you're getting in between. Instead of liberating you, a LIB holds you back from ever achieving the simplicity, happiness, and fulfillment that comes from having a life in balance.

SO WHAT'S YOUR LIB?

I know my own LIBs—or, I should say, the ones that used to run my life. I'm an addict who got treated for alcohol and drug abuse. But after I surrendered to those two LIBs and stopped abusing them, I turned to other LIBs, including relationship addiction, eating disorders, and workaholism, all in pursuit of perfection. I wanted to have the best body possible to attract as many people as possible. I sought attention through relationships, trying to feel a connection with anyone I could so that I could feel some sense of self-worth. I worked multiple jobs putting in seventy-hour weeks trying to earn as much money as possible. I thought the key to happiness after quitting alcohol and drugs was having as many people around me as I could and as much money in the bank as possible, yet I was never happy. That's because all of these behaviors were just new LIBs pulling me more and more out of balance.

Now it's your turn. Figuring out what your LIB may be is as easy as reviewing the ADAPT list in chapter 2. Many of the conditions listed there (being abusive; suffering from a disorder; having an addiction; being greedy, lazy, or jealous; feeling harmful emotions such as rejection or inferiority) are LIBs, since they are all clearly negative behaviors.

Other conditions on the ADAPT list may not be obvious LIBs but could be tied to something deeper that is spinning you out of balance indirectly. Take someone in denial about losing his hair. Or someone in denial about having a massive caffeine addiction. Aren't hair loss and caffeine addiction quite common? Can these seemingly harmless LIBs really pull a life out of balance? The answer is yes.

The person in denial about losing his hair may end up avoiding certain healthy situations—like a fun party, a dream date, or any opportunity to meet new people—just because he doesn't feel comfortable about his appearance and can't admit it. And the person in denial about being addicted to caffeine must be overly tired for a reason, whether lack of sleep or a need for an extra boost of energy to keep on top of her job or other nonstop demands in her life. The point is, if you're in denial about any item on the ADAPT list, that's something having an effect on your life in some way—and not a healthy way.

THE THREE KINDS OF LIBS

Some LIBs can be silly, annoying little habits, while others can be serious issues that immediately threaten your life. That's why I like to break LIBs up into three categories: passive, aggressive, and severe.

Passive LIBs

A passive LIB is a common, simple, negative behavior that poses no direct threat to your health, lifestyle, or relationships. However, it steals time that you could be spending doing healthier things. Most passive LIBs don't carry much stigma to them—if any at all—because typically they are common habits that most people share. On a scale of 1 to 10, this type of LIB falls between 1 and 3.

Examples of passive LIBs include

- Mild computer addiction (texting, compulsive Web surfing, eBay addiction, etc.)

- Video game addiction (or excessive TV watching)

- Caffeine addiction

- Negative personality traits such as procrastination, greediness, jealousy, or stubbornness

Aggressive LIBs

An aggressive LIB is a moderately negative behavior that could affect your health, your lifestyle, or your relationships over time. It falls between a passive LIB and a severe LIB in terms of seriousness. On the LIB scale of 1 to 10, these LIBs fall between 4 and 7.

Examples of aggressive LIBs include

- Major computer addiction (cybersex, online affairs, etc.)

- Financial irresponsibility

- Nicotine addiction

- Sexual compulsion

- Infidelity

- Trust issues

- Losing passion for someone or something

- Feeling inferior

- Feeling rejected

- Problem gambling

- Lack of accountability

- Work addiction

- Being forced to ignore your true sexuality

- Debilitating phobias

- Ignoring minor physical health issues (poor hygiene, a dermatological issue, vision problems, etc.)

- Ignoring minor mental health issues (OCD, postpartum depression, panic attacks, etc.)

- Negative personality traits such as maliciousness, excessive infatuation, prejudice, or arrogance

- Being codependent

- Ignoring LIBs in someone you care about

- Ignoring being an abuser

- Ignoring that you may need part- or full-time assisted living

- Any of your passive LIBs that's affecting the health, lifestyle, or relationships of someone else

Severe LIBs

A severe LIB is any negative behavior so destructive it poses an immediate danger to the denier's health—or that of someone else. On the LIB scale of 1 to 10, severe LIBs fall between 9 and 10. The denier who uses these LIBs is a ticking time bomb—every second spent wasted in denial literally brings the person one step closer to death. When I do interventions, it's usually on deniers who engage in severe LIBs and are months away from dying—if not weeks or sometimes days—owing to their denial of their LIB.

Examples of severe LIBs include

- Alcoholism

- Substance abuse

- Food addiction/eating disorder

- Ignoring a major physical health issue (high blood pressure, cancer, diabetes, etc.)

- Ignoring a major mental health issue (major depression, bipolar disorder, dementia, etc.)

- Ignoring being abused

HAVE YOU FOUND YOUR LIB YET?

You have? Congratulations! Know that the lessons in this book will help you put an end to it. If you haven't found your LIB yet, that's okay. As you continue to read this book, you will eventually figure out—with my help and your own honesty—what your LIB is. This book is designed over the next few chapters to teach you everything you need to know about denial, to show you how to monitor your life, and, finally, to show you how to ask those around you for help. Somewhere along this journey, I promise you, we will figure out what your LIB is. Then I'll show you how to remove it from your life for good.

However, I need you to promise me something: if you know what your LIB is right now, or if you discover what your LIB is in the next few chapters, keep reading this book and don't skip to part 3. Even though you may think these next few chapters no longer pertain to you, they may be what ultimately gets your life back in balance. That's because many deniers suffer from not just one LIB but several at once. Just because you discovered one of your LIBs early in this book doesn't mean there aren't more lingering in your life. Reading this book straight through will help you begin to discover each and every one of them.

4

Why We Deny

At its root, denial may be a defense mechanism that we all use to shield ourselves from the things we don't want to face head-on, but we don't all share the same motives for using it. There are many different reasons why our brains—or should I say "we"—decide to place ourselves in a state of denial about our problems and our LIBs. That being said, nearly everyone prefers to stay in denial for one—or several—of the following eight reasons:

1. We're looking to avoid the work.

2. We don't want to feel vulnerable or out of control.

3. We fear the blame.

4. We don't know the first step to take.

5. We don't think our problem is a problem.

6. The problem isn't creating a "bottom" for us.

7. We're enabled by those around us.

8. We believe that ignoring a problem can make it go away.

Which one of the eight is your reason for staying in denial? That's not always an easy question to answer, especially if you don't believe you're in denial in the first place. Your answer may also depend on a series of individual factors, ranging from who you are as a person to how you were raised, your work ethic, where you are with your self-esteem, and even the type of people you surround yourself with on a regular basis. Because of all these factors, you could be in denial for more than one of these reasons at the same time.

If you're in denial for more than one reason, breaking you out of denial's spell will take a little more effort. There may be one main reason why you deny, but your additional reasons are like extra layers of bricks added to your wall. Each additional reason can make you more skeptical about your decision to break out of denial, giving you more justification for staying hidden behind your wall.

Even if you still don't believe that you're in denial, having a full grasp of all eight reasons why people deny may mark a turning point for you. You see, to begin accepting the possibility that you are in denial about something, it's essential to understand why your mind would bother to hide certain things from you in the first place. Here's a rundown of the reasons you may be in denial and why this book can help you overcome each one.

WE'RE LOOKING TO AVOID THE WORK

Deep down, most deniers assume that facing their own denial—and tackling the issues it's hiding and protecting them from—is a huge endeavor. They fear the major decisions they may have to make if they confront it. They worry about the disruptions to their life and all the changes and choices that may be associated with fixing those issues. Staying in denial lets deniers turn a blind eye to all of that effort, so that they can go about their less-complicated lives—even though the reality is that denial is making life far more complicated for them than it has to be.

I'm going to be just as honest with you as I am with my clients. It is well within your power to defeat denial, but it's not something that happens easily without rolling up your sleeves and putting in the effort. However, that doesn't mean it always has to be difficult. If being apprehensive about the work involved is your reason for staying in denial, the tools in this book will help you break out of denial by making it somewhat easier than it would be doing it on your own. I'll show you a few simple strategies that will prepare you to face whatever you're in denial about.

WE DON'T WANT TO FEEL VULNERABLE OR OUT OF CONTROL

Many of the things we may hate about ourselves and wish we could change—from those extra few pounds we carry around to our fear of things like heights, snakes, spiders, and such—are actually our body's way of protecting us and keeping us safe from harm.

Did you know that the reason your body always carries a few extra pounds is to ensure that you'll have enough stored body fat to survive? Did you know that your heart races when you're confronted by something you fear because it is instantly raising your levels of adrenaline and intake of oxygen to make sure you have enough stamina and alertness to run away from the danger you may be facing? Your body is perpetually protecting itself with a series of defense responses that can sometimes be more hindrance than help, depending on your goals.

The mind turns to denial to protect itself—and you—in a similar way. When you feel emotionally vulnerable or not in control of your life, it's usually because you're afraid of how your life might change if you dared to address the negative issue in your life—even if the change is for the better. That's when denial sometimes steps in to help create a feeling of self-assurance. It creates an illusion that lets you falsely believe that everything's perfectly fine with your life. It keeps you safe, comfortable, and grounded so that you never have to face a situation or make an important decision that might unravel that cocoon of comfort.

Our bodies may be designed to protect us to ensure our survival, but that doesn't always mean we want them to. The good news is that you can counteract your body's instincts if you follow the right program. Just as you can lose those last few pounds around your middle with the right diet and exercise program, and just as you can overcome any fear with the right counseling, this book will show you the right tools to use to keep your mind from reaching for denial whenever it feels helpless and exposed.

WE FEAR THE BLAME

Regardless of how honest we may be with ourselves about the mistakes we make in life, none of us ever feel good about making them. Admitting that your life—or someone else's life—is dysfunctional because of a few wrong choices you made along the way is a hard pill for anyone to swallow. For example, I once had a client who chose to ignore her failing marriage rather than own up to the fact that her problem with being obsessive-compulsive was tearing it apart. I've witnessed countless others who preferred to deny having a drinking problem, being depressive, falling into debt, and many other LIBs, to avoid the shame they thought they would suffer by admitting their actions.

We fear the overwhelming sense of guilt that will haunt us if we're finally forced to take responsibility for decisions we made in our past—decisions that may be damaging our present and our future. We fear those who, pointing their fingers in our direction, might judge us if we bring our flaws out into the light for everyone to see. That's why it's much simpler to deny that anything is wrong and allow it to get worse, rather than admit that there is chaos in our lives and accept responsibility for our own actions.

That fear of judgment can also keep some people from recognizing—or addressing—a LIB in someone they love. Some people may choose to stay in denial of someone else's LIB because they act the same way themselves. For example, parents may remain in denial of their child's drinking problem because they also drink excessively. Even if they desperately want to get their child help, they know that any such help might result in the finger of blame being pointed at themselves and then having to address their own LIB.

It's almost impossible to point out someone else's LIB when you know in your heart that person can say the same to you—and quite possibly blame you for modeling the problematic LIB in the first place. At the very least, pointing out someone else's LIB under these circumstances is risky. Instead, it's much easier to ignore the other person's LIB so that he or she will ignore yours. It's a silent, unspoken bond of denial.

Using the tools in this book, you'll learn to not just accept but embrace what it is that you've been in denial about in your life. The process may sound humiliating to you, but I can assure you that it's actually the opposite. Owning up to what you're in denial about and taking action against the denial instantly earns respect—not accusations—from those in your life, especially those closest to you.

If it's your own guilt that you fear, then finally doing something about it will ease that guilt once and for all.

WE DON'T KNOW THE FIRST STEP TO TAKE

For some deniers, it's not that they don't want to deal with their problems—it's that they don't know how. It's easier for some individuals to slip into a state of "half-denial": they remain aware of their LIB, but convince themselves that they don't know the right course of action to take to address it.

In today's information age, it's not difficult to find a few solutions to try that might help you overcome denial. But I'll admit that it's not always easy to know which works best. Maybe you're confused about your options—or maybe you choose to stay confused because you're too embarrassed to ask anyone what your first step should be. Regardless of your reasoning, this book incorporates—and simplifies—many of the proven strategies used by counselors as well as by professional interventionists, such as myself. These strategies will guide you effortlessly from the very first step to the last.

WE DON'T THINK OUR PROBLEM IS A PROBLEM

Some people innocently sit in denial about their LIBs because they fail to see that their behaviors are in any way abnormal. This can happen for several reasons.

1. Your LIBs May Be What You Grew Up With

Certain behaviors, no matter how disruptive they are, can seem conventional if they've been present in your life since the day you were born. How you were raised by your parents—and who was present in your life as you developed from childhood to adulthood—can have an important effect on what you consider "normal" behavior.

For some deniers, watching their parents, relatives, siblings, or childhood friends engaging in acts of destructive behavior and being regularly exposed to those behaviors while growing up can make it difficult to recognize that those behaviors are abnormal when they see those behaviors in the present. For example, if you grew up with an abusive parent, you might not think your anger issues are a problem when they bubble to the surface in your life and someone points them out. If your mother was obsessed with keeping her weight under control, you may not think your strict dietary habits suggest a borderline eating disorder. Because deniers' home environments allowed their behaviors to flourish, they innocently may not recognize their LIB as a problem, even when they step outside the safety of their family boundaries.

2. Your LIBs May Be Part of Your Culture

I've worked with many clients who truly thought it was entirely fine to drink excessively because of their Irish descent. I've handled other clients who honestly believed it was acceptable to lose their temper because they were Italian. I've even had clients who assumed it was okay to be promiscuous and cheat on their spouse because they were Latin. What do all these drunken Irish, hot-tempered Italians, and Latin lovers have in common? They believe their bad behaviors are acceptable because the behavior is tied to their ethnicity.

Many people believe that some cultures have certain LIBs attached to them, but most—if not all—of these notions are nothing more than stereotypes. Is it really more excusable for people of certain cultures to consume larger quantities of liquor simply because it's what they're expected to do? Are people of certain races allowed to behave in irresponsible, life-damaging ways based on nothing more than their ancestry? The answer is no. But if you believe that your ethnicity comes with certain quirks that make unacceptable behavior somehow acceptable, you'll be more likely to stay in denial of those behaviors that are putting your life out of balance.

It doesn't matter what behaviors you grew up with or what ethnicity you are. The fact of the matter is that you deserve better than to engage in whatever LIBs you're excusing as normal behavior. I promise you that your life isn't any better for including those LIBs, but if denial is preventing you from seeing that right now, try to look past yourself for a second. Instead, look at the lives of either the family members you learned your LIB from or others in your culture who engage in the same LIB. Do they seem happy, fulfilled, and in balance? I'm willing to bet the answer is no, and if you're imitating their actions, then that's why the answer is no for you as well.

You may be dismissing your LIB because of your family history or heritage, but you're using it for an entirely different reason. If those around you are the reason you can't see that you're in denial and can't see why your LIB is unhealthy, then you may not be able to find enough help close to home to beat it.

OUR PROBLEM ISN'T CREATING A "BOTTOM" FOR US

Deniers who suffer from a severe type of LIB, such as a hard-core, life-threatening addiction, find it much easier to remain in denial as long as they don't hit what counselors and specialists refer to as "rock bottom." Hitting bottom happens when deniers' behaviors and actions damage their lives to such a drastic extent that they are left with absolutely no choice but to address their LIBs. As long as deniers can still function in their lives without anything earth-shattering happening, they can stay in denial.

There are five types of rock bottom that deniers may experience, depending on their LIB:

1. They may hit a *health bottom:* The denier is confronted with failing health and left with no choice but to either stop the LIB or die.

2. They may hit an *emotional bottom:* The denier has pushed away so many people that the emotional strain becomes too great to bear.

3. They may hit a *legal bottom:* The law intervenes because the denier's LIB has caused him or her to break the law or to be threatened or charged with some form of legal action. This leaves the denier with no choice but to end the LIB or face criminal charges.

4. They may hit a personal *financial bottom:* Having used up all his or her resources—money, possessions—on the LIB, the denier is left with little recourse but to face it.

5. They may hit a *spiritual bottom:* This is a personal experience between the denier and his or her God. This type of bottom varies from person to person, but it usually takes the form of an epiphany that changes the denier's whole mind-set and drives him or her to seek a better spiritual place.

If you discover that you suffer from a passive or aggressive LIB—which most of us do—the tools in this book can help you break your denial without ever needing to hit a bottom. But if you suffer from a severe LIB that's too strong to break using the tools in this book, you may need professional assistance. If that's the case for you, I will show you in a later chapter who you should turn to for information, support, and guidance when denial is impossible to break on your own.

WE'RE ENABLED BY THOSE AROUND US

Sometimes deniers are completely unaware of their negative actions because those closest to them are allowing their behavior to go unnoticed or they're covering up the damage the deniers are doing to themselves and others around them. For example,

- I've worked with people who denied having anger issues and never realized they had a problem because everyone around them was always apologizing for upsetting them.

- I've done many interventions with people who denied that they drank too much and whose spouses believed that they deserved a drink after a stressful day at work.

- I've known people who were in denial about being financially irresponsible and who never saw themselves as having a problem because their parents or spouse kept refilling their bank accounts or paying off their debts.

If you're this kind of denier, you may discover that the same people who are covering for you are whispering to each other behind your back about your actions and how hurtful they are. But if they never tell you what they're feeling, it's quite possible for you to remain oblivious to the impact of your actions.

The tools I'm going to teach you are aimed not just at your own denial but also at those who may be causing your denial to flourish. I'll show you how to get those who are enabling you to recognize their own contribution to your LIB, so that they will stop refueling it and start helping you to extinguish it. I'll also show you how to pull together a new set of people to help support you. Once you handpick a tight-knit "circle of trust," you'll have a constant and sturdy source of support in your efforts to beat denial.

WE BELIEVE THAT IGNORING A PROBLEM CAN MAKE IT GO AWAY

There are some people who choose denial because they truly feel that ignorance is bliss. I've seen this reaction from people who have found themselves stuck in a bad relationship but who believe in their heart that things will simply turn around and get better one day if they just stick it out. I've seen this reaction from many parents who, in denial about their child's bad behaviors, tell themselves things like "It's just a phase he'll soon grow out of."

But denial isn't a salesman knocking on your door who you can sit quietly and wait out until he walks away. Whatever LIB you're in denial about sits at your door like a salesman who has all the time in the world for you. Hoping the LIB will eventually disappear, instead of opening the door to face it, only ensures that while it's staying put on your porch you can't step outside and experience a healthier life for yourself.

Wishing your problems would just go away on their own may not be entirely wise, but if you think you are this kind of denier, it does tell me something you're going to like to hear. It means you're aware that there's some type of LIB in your life right now and that it isn't going away on its own. Even if you're afraid to stand up to your denial, you've made a terrific start because you already recognize that there's a problem that needs to be solved. I'll show you how to finally open the door and confront denial face-to-face so that it's less likely to come knocking again.

5

The Six Types of Denial That Spell Denial

Knowing the reasons *why* we deny is an important step toward accepting that we are all in denial about something. But understanding *how* we deny can make it much easier to recognize why routinely using this natural coping mechanism isn't a healthy response. This understanding can also teach you how to recognize the warning signs that you're in denial about something in your life.

There are six distinct and unique ways in which we deny:

- *Denying:* Completely repressing or refuting that we have any tangible problem to address

- *Event manipulation:* Acknowledging our LIB, but not recognizing its repeated occurrence

- *Neglect:* Recognizing our LIB but ignoring the fact that what we're doing—or what's being done to us—is in any way hurtful to ourselves or others

- *Interference:* Blaming something that chemically affects our judgment, such as a drug, alcohol, a mood, or an existing medical condition, instead of ourselves

- *Alteration:* Placing all or part of the blame for our actions on someone or something else

- *Lying:* Changing the facts or lying about our LIB

Before I explain each of these forms of denial in full, I first need to stress a few important points about all six in general. Although each of the six is unhealthy, some can be more dangerous than others. Which forms of denial are potentially the most harmful to your life is hard to say, since it differs depending on the individual and the LIB you are using denial to protect.

If you take the first letter of each type of denial, you'll notice that collectively they spell DENIAL. I present them in this order to help you remember all six; that way, you can instantly recognize each one, either in yourself or in others, and immediately know what to expect. But be aware that even though all six together spell DENIAL, it only takes one to put you in denial.

Another thing to know about the six types of denial is that they can be used individually or collectively, depending on the LIB and the denier. It's quite possible for some deniers to use more than one form of denial to hide their actions, which makes it much harder to remove denial from their lives. Each type of denial comes with its own set of bricks to help you fortify your wall. The more forms of denial you use to build your wall, the thicker it becomes—and the more tools it takes to tear it down brick by brick. Understanding all six will give you the insight you need to recognize each form of denial within yourself, so you can defeat them all.

DENIAL BY DENYING

Denial by denying is a person's complete refusal to admit that there is any problem to address. These deniers remain in a permanent state of ignorance when it comes to all thoughts, facts, and events related to their actions—or someone else's actions—in an attempt to completely shield themselves from ever having to address the issue.

One of the toughest interventions I ever had to do was with a young man who suffered from alcohol abuse. He had lost job after job, as well as the respect of many of his friends and family members. Because of the extent of his chronic drinking and the toll it had taken on his body, he was also, in my estimation, weeks away from death. You would think that having all these factors in his face would have opened his eyes to the problem, but that was the scary part. His eyes were wide open, but his denial was so strong that his mind refused to connect the dots between his drinking and his crumbling life.

People who use this type of denial truly don't see any aspect of the big picture. Instead, they keep themselves completely blind to their LIB and to anything that might be wrong in their lives, even when everybody around them can see it and is trying to explain or present it to them. They refute what they're being told because they simply don't believe it's real and occurring in their world. This form of denial is almost like being in a state of dementia—what is reality for everyone else is not reality to the denier. Instead, it's either

- Not happening

- Something that never happened

- Something that never happened in the way others describe
  it (the denier may recognize what's going on, but his or her
  perception of the incident, feelings, or actions isn't the same
  as everyone else's)

This type of denial often is found in those who have experienced—or are experiencing—something so extremely difficult to cope with that pretending it doesn't exist is simply the only way to continue functioning. Here are some examples of such denial, based on the ADAPT (Abuse, Disorders, Addiction, Physical issues, and the Truth) list from chapter 2:

- *Abuse:* A woman doesn't remember being molested because her mind has caused her to forget the incident.

- *Disorders:* A man who completely denies being afraid to fly convinces himself that he loves to drive cross-country, instead of facing his fear.

- *Addiction:* A drug user may never remember taking drugs. I once knew a drug addict who was thoroughly convinced that he wasn't using heroin. When asked about the track marks running up both his arms and between his toes, he honestly believed it must have been done to him in his sleep.

- *Physical issues:* A patient diagnosed with cancer is thoroughly convinced that the doctor is absolutely wrong.

- *The Truth:* A homosexual man continues to date people of the opposite sex because he's convinced that he is straight.

Others may find themselves using this type of denial when those they love are using a LIB or experiencing something that the denier can't handle. These deniers don't lie to change the facts or events that took place but simply refuse to believe the person they love is dealing with anything painful and life-imbalancing—despite the mounting evidence right in front of their eyes. Examples include

- *Abuse:* A mother refuses to believe her child is being abused by her husband, even after seeing the bruises for herself.

- *Disorders:* A father can't admit that his child may have a learning disability, despite hearing concern from teachers and family members. The most painful example I ever witnessed was in a wealthy family whose little girl clearly suffered from dyslexia. Because the parents lived their lives in a perfect bubble, they refused to accept that their daughter could have anything wrong with her and instead chose to blame the teachers, tutors, and anyone else associated with her learning.

- *Addiction:* A woman unconditionally denies that her friend uses drugs, despite the fact that the friend was caught by the police using drugs.

- *Physical issues:* The parents of a child who is clinically obese refuse to acknowledge the problem, even after being told by a physician.

- *The Truth:* Confronted with evidence of his wife's infidelity, a husband refuses to believe he's been cheated on.

Denial by denying is the most lethal of the six types of denial. After all, if you can't even see the problem in your life (such as a stressful situation, an emotional struggle, or an unhealthy LIB), how can you begin to handle it?

The process of breaking this type of denial is similar to that for the other five types I'm about to reveal to you, but the treatment is drastically different. It typically takes a lot more medication, therapy, and work with a licensed professional to break down the wall of someone who denies by denying. It may take years before these deniers realize what was done to them that has brought their LIB to the surface. There is usually something within a person in this type of denial that requires serious medical attention.

If You Recognize That You've Been Denying by Denial . . .

Congratulations! You're no longer in denial!

Ah, if only it were that easy. Unfortunately, those who rely on this type of denial don't instantly recognize it just by reading about it.

DENIAL BY EVENT MANIPULATION

Those in denial by event manipulation acknowledge their LIB but don't recognize the habitual nature of their actions. Instead, they believe their LIB is either a onetime event or a rare occurrence that happens every so often. They shrink the numbers on how often they turn to—or someone else uses—the LIB.

Once again based on the ADAPT list, here are some examples of denial by event manipulation:

- *Abuse:* A mother regularly berates her children but only owns up to crossing the line a few times.

- *Disorders:* A person who hoards insists that he only saves a few things, instead of admitting that he can't throw anything away.

- *Addiction:* Years back, I worked with a young alcoholic who claimed that she only drank on the weekends. In reality, she drank every day but only got completely drunk on the weekends.

- *Physical issues:* A person suffers with chronic pain but only recognizes it at times when it's too much to bear.

- *The Truth:* An individual is stubborn with every one of his decisions but only recognizes a handful of times when his pigheadedness spiraled out of control.

To make it easier to fudge the numbers in their heads, some people divide the problem they're in denial about (whether it's an issue or a LIB) into smaller pieces so that they never see the problem as a whole. I've noticed this phenomenon in most problem gamblers. I had one client who was a master at convincing himself that he didn't have a problem by saying such things as

> "Playing cards every week with my friends isn't a problem because everyone does that!"

> "Jumping on the Internet to play a few money games on a poker site isn't a problem because everyone does that!"

> "Betting part of my paycheck on this week's office pool game isn't a problem because everyone does that!"

By breaking up his LIB, he was able to run through a series of actions that never added up in his brain—so he never saw the total sum of his actions.

Here are more examples, using the ADAPT list:

- *Abuse:* A psychologically abusive woman doesn't single out any one person with her attacks but makes random negative comments to anyone she meets.

- *Disorders:* A man who suffers from body dysmorphia obsesses on random body parts throughout the day, instead of recognizing that he is obsessed with his entire appearance.

- *Addiction:* I've known substance abusers who used a variety of different drugs, instead of sticking with one, so that they never felt dependent on any one of them.

- *Physical issues:* A woman in denial about being underweight won't let herself piece together that her low resistance to infections, chronic fatigue, and loss of menstruation are all related to not eating enough.

- *The Truth:* Someone in denial about having envy issues never focuses on one person but envies everyone around him, including people he doesn't know.

Other deniers who use event manipulation divide their LIB into pieces but decide that certain pieces are far more serious than others. That way, they only count as serious the times when they completely lose control of their LIB, not the times when they have their LIB partially under control.

For instance, many of my clients with a drug addiction see themselves as having a problem only when they completely mess up and go on a weeklong bender. One client didn't count as having an issue with drugs his routine of sitting at home smoking marijuana every night. Popping a few prescription pills in the morning to wake himself up for the day somehow didn't count as being part of a much bigger problem. Because his perception of what he considered a LIB was attached to the extreme, he simply discounted anything that didn't match that level of severity.

Having categorized which actions are bad and which are good, deniers by event manipulation can engage in the same LIB all day long, add up only the bad occurrences and ignore the acceptable ones, and conclude that they don't have a problem. This type of denial can be used in every example in the ADAPT list:

- *Abuse:* A domestic abuser doesn't count the times when he berates his family and only sees that he has a problem when he actually hits someone.

- *Disorders:* A person with separation anxiety ignores her mood swings, tantrums, persistent worrying, repeated nightmares, and recurring nausea, but acknowledges her LIB when she frantically calls others for help.

- *Addiction:* Someone with a work addiction won't admit that her habit of working ten-hour days is affecting her life, but sees the problem when she misses an important event in her child's life.

- *Physical issues:* A person with high blood pressure ignores his constant headaches and blurred vision, but takes these symptoms seriously when they're severe enough to land him in the hospital.

- *The Truth:* A jealous woman disregards her constant nagging of those she dates and the distrust she shows them, but recognizes her LIB when it causes a breakup.

If You Recognize That You've Been Denying by Event Manipulation . . .

Remember that even a few occurrences of a LIB amount to one too many, especially if the results you're adding up every once in a while are extreme. The fact that you can even include in your calculations a handful of times a LIB has gotten out of control is a definite sign that there's a problem.

To be honest, most people don't have extreme moments like the ones you choose to count unless they have a problem. Using the examples I've just mentioned, those who aren't abusive can't count the few times they hit someone—because they never have. And those who don't have high blood pressure can't count how many times they've been hospitalized for it—because that's never happened to them.

DENIAL BY NEGLECT

Those who deny by neglect recognize their problems or bad behaviors but simply ignore the fact that what they're doing—or what's being done to them—is in any way hurtful or harmful to themselves or others. Simply put, these deniers neglect to take their situation seriously enough.

Those who deny in this way remain oblivious to the seriousness of their dilemma. They don't believe that their LIB—or someone else's LIB—is having negative consequences for anyone, despite the damage it's done to their health, finances, and well-being. Here are examples of denial by neglect based on the ADAPT list:

- *Abuse:* A battered husband makes light of the continual beatings he suffers at the hands of his wife.

- *Disorders:* A woman whose LIB is obsessive cleaning fails to see that her actions are keeping her from spending quality time with her family.

- *Addiction:* A lifelong smoker thinks his two-pack-a-day habit affects no one but himself, and he doesn't see that his children are daily victims of secondhand smoke.

- *Physical issues:* A woman who suffers from being overweight refuses to believe that her actions are related in any way to her aching joints, high blood pressure, and constant fatigue.

- *The Truth:* A person with a deep infatuation for a co-worker thinks that his persistent advances are innocent and playful when, in actuality, they may border on sexual harassment.

Some people find themselves in denial by neglect because they haven't yet taken the time to step back and assess the full damage caused by their LIB. Another reason for denial by neglect can be seen in the case of the denier who is being shielded from the consequences of his LIB by someone who is enabling him—perhaps a loved one who's silently paying the denier's bills or making excuses for him to friends and family. Regardless of why they choose to remain unconcerned, deniers by neglect simply don't believe that their actions or the situation they're in could hurt them or anyone else.

It can be even more difficult to snap someone out of denial by neglect if the individual has a LIB that is admired and rewarded by society. When all you hear from outsiders is nothing but admiration and applause for your actions, it is much more difficult to believe a loved one warning you that your LIB is hazardous. For example:

- *Abuse:* Fortunately, abuse is never admired, so you generally don't see examples from this category.

- *Disorders:* Someone in denial about being obsessive-compulsive is constantly praised by others for being incredibly organized.

- *Addiction:* A workaholic in denial is the envy of all his co-workers for his job performance and frequent successes.

- *Physical issues:* A woman in denial about being dangerously underweight hears comments from others every day about how lean and model-like she looks.

- *The Truth:* An excessively greedy man is constantly reminded by others that he is lucky to have so many possessions.

Positive reinforcement can make this form of denial difficult to handle. When your LIB has an ego-boosting effect on one part of your life, it's even harder to see that other parts of your life are diminished because of it. I knew a workaholic who spent seventy hours at his job each and every week. This CEO enjoyed seeing his bank accounts growing and considered himself on top of his game because of his unyielding dedication, yet he had no idea that neglect was causing his friendships and his relationships with his wife and kids to slip away.

Denial may highlight the ego-boosting quality of your actions—more money, being the life of the party, having a lean body, having everything you've ever wanted—while blinding you to the LIB responsible for your apparent successes (being a workaholic, being an alcoholic, being an exercise bulimic, being bankrupt). All you notice are the few positive things in your life instead of the countless negative things.

This type of denial can go a step further. In addition to being unfazed by their LIB, or even believing that it's good for them, some deniers may be convinced that putting a stop to their LIB, or addressing someone else's, will spin their life out of balance. For example:

- *Abuse:* A woman in denial about being abused insists that broaching the subject will only make her abuser angrier and crueler.

- *Disorders:* An individual with an eating disorder says, "I can't eat a lot of food! I have bad genetics, and I'll balloon up if I don't watch my weight!"

- *Addiction:* A man addicted to caffeine insists that his work performance will suffer tremendously if he doesn't keep himself alert with his two-pot-a-day habit.

- *Physical issues:* A person with a serious health issue dismisses the idea of having it checked out because he doesn't want anyone to get upset or to worry about him.

- *The Truth:* Someone who is procrastinating about looking for another job justifies her laziness by saying that things at her current job are shaky and, if she focuses on job-hunting too soon, she may get fired as a result.

By convincing themselves that addressing their denial will only make things worse, people who use this type of denial can be much harder to reach. They see their LIB as something that's helping to prevent chaos or to maintain control over something that's important to them. Getting them to notice that their LIB is having the opposite effect takes work, but it's nothing the tools in this book can't handle.

If You Recognize That You've Been Denying by Neglect . . .

Know that not everything is quite what it seems. If you're a denier who believes your LIB isn't having a hugely negative effect on your life, that's only because you haven't done a final tally of all the damage yet. If you're a denier who receives heaps of praise and admiration for your LIB, I'm sure that those who care for you probably have a completely different opinion. Finally, if you're a denier who fears that your life will plunge horribly out of control if you confront or remove your LIB, the truth is that, by keeping your LIB, what you fear most is already happening to you.

No matter which of the three forms of denial by neglect you may be in, you'll learn to see your LIB for what it really is and come to understand that replacing it for something healthier will only change your life for the better.

DENIAL BY INTERFERENCE

Maybe you've heard others, or even yourself, say things such as

"I never meant to do that. I was just high and things got out of hand."

"That wasn't me talking . . . it was the booze."

"I'm bipolar, so I can't help it when I lash out like that."

"I'm not prejudiced. That word came out just because I'm feeling stressed today."

"I'm not really infatuated with him. I was just feeling lonely and depressed that night."

To deny by interference is to blame a negative outcome on something that chemically affected your judgment, such as a drug, alcohol, a mood, or a medical condition, instead of yourself. The denier claims to have been in a different mental or physical state at the time and therefore shouldn't be held responsible, or made to pay in any way, for his or her inappropriate actions.

Here are some examples of denial by interference:

- *Abuse:* A bully hits someone at a party and blames his violence on being drunk.

- *Disorders:* A mother with postpartum depression tells others that her sleeping medication is making her feel less energetic.

- *Addiction:* A gambler claims that he lost all his money at the casinos because they serve free liquor.

- *Physical issues:* An obese woman tells people she has a thyroid problem, when what she really has is a food addiction.

- *The Truth:* An unfaithful husband admits that he cheated at a bachelor party, but only because he had too much to drink.

Many people who use denial by interference don't have an addiction problem or a medical issue. The LIBs associated with addiction and medical conditions are just a convenient excuse when they need something to blame. Other people who use denial by interference fall into two camps: those who suffer from more than one LIB, and those who pretend to have a second LIB to cover up the one they really have.

Deniers with more than one LIB will often shift the blame onto whichever LIB they think is less severe when they do something inappropriate. For example, someone who's in denial about both being an alcoholic and being abusive might blame a violent outburst on whatever he had to drink that night. That way, if he suffers any consequences, he can use one LIB (his alcoholism) to deflect attention from the other LIB (his abusive nature), which he knows is a much more serious problem.

When a denier pretends to have one LIB to cover up for another one, it's usually because the LIB he or she does suffer from is mortifying or embarrassing. For example, I knew a sex addict who claimed she had a drug problem when she was finally caught acting out sexually. I've even seen someone with a panic disorder claim that he was drunk after crashing his car, instead of confessing that he had an unexpected panic episode. Typically, denial by interference—which is also a form of denial by lying—is found in deniers who suffer from severe LIBs.

After all, why would anyone admit to something they didn't do unless what they did do was far worse?

DENIAL BY ALTERATION

Denial by alteration is placing either part or all of the blame for your actions on someone or something else. These deniers deflect the blame onto something that "forced" them to resort to their LIB. They live by this simple rule: "It's not my fault . . . it's your fault."

One of the worst situations I've ever experienced with denial by alteration happened while performing an intervention on a man whose LIB was meth addiction and alcoholism. In the middle of the intervention, he had a psychotic break and began saying incredibly hurtful things, threatened to kill his father, and became so violent that he was maced, arrested, placed in handcuffs, and taken away to spend three weeks in a psych ward. When he came out, he denied that his actions had had anything to do with his LIB. Instead, he said he lost his temper because he was pushed into treatment. His denial let him believe that every single one of his disruptive actions that day had been the fault of everyone around him—and not himself.

Here are some other examples of denial by alteration, based once again on the ADAPT list:

- *Abuse:* A husband in denial about being abusive blames his wife for the fact that he's been yelling at her by claiming she said or did something that set him off.

- *Disorders:* A woman in denial about being antisocial criticizes others for not inviting her to certain events or not trying hard enough to be her friend.

- *Addiction:* A man in denial about eating too much blames his spouse for cooking big meals or keeping high-calorie food in the house.

- *Physical issues:* A person in denial about losing her hearing accuses the people talking to her of speaking too softly or not clearly enough.

- *The Truth:* Someone in denial about being in financial debt claims he was tricked into signing up with the wrong credit card company.

Deniers who use this type of denial don't always deflect the blame onto the victim of their LIB. They may even pass the buck of blame to people who aren't anywhere near them.

In my business, I've heard every deflection in the book. Here are just a few examples that my clients have used:

"I'm not violent. I'm just a hotheaded Italian."

"Everyone in my family cries out of the blue for no reason. It's normal."

"I like to drink. So what, I'm Irish!"

"I don't have an eating disorder. I just come from an overweight family."

"My dad told me that joke. I'm not a racist."

When people claim they're merely copying the behaviors of people they're close to or related to, it's denial by alteration. Instead of addressing their own LIB, they deny that it's a problem, because they see it merely as an extension of someone else's problem.

Another tactic sometimes used by those who rely on this form of denial is to inflict additional pain on anyone who dares to approach them about their LIB, through either anger or abusive behavior. When confronted, the denier reacts in an unpleasant manner in an effort to scare or shock the accusers. This often happens in the interventions that I do. I've also seen deniers threaten to take something away so that their accusers feel they have something to lose should they dare to bring up the topic again. The aim of both approaches is to make other people less likely to approach the denier in the future or to upset them enough to stop caring as much.

If You Recognize That You've Been Denying
by Alteration . . .

No matter what you think and no matter how you feel, your LIB is triggered by only one thing, and that's you. You own your LIB, just as every single person you've ever accused of triggering it has their own LIB to contend with.

Here's the thing: as much as you may want to shift the blame for your actions onto others, owning up to what's really your problem gives you more control over your efforts to remove it from your life for good. When something belongs to you outright, it's yours to do with however you please, because you have 100 percent full control over it.

DENIAL BY LYING

A person who denies by lying changes the facts, or avoids them entirely, by lying about certain facts in order to lessen the severity of the situation. Using the ADAPT list, I can give you some examples of denial by lying:

- *Abuse:* A woman claims that the bruises on her arms are from falling down at home—when in fact they were inflicted by another person.

- *Disorders:* A young man tells his friends he just bought the new shirt he's wearing when actually he stole it from a store the day before.

- *Addiction:* A husband claims that his wife's snoring keeps him awake instead of confessing that he looks tired from partying, playing video games, surfing the Web, or working throughout the night.

- *Physical issues:* A woman tells her partner that the rash around her mouth is a food allergy when it's actually a symptom of an STD.

- *The Truth:* A woman ignores her ringing phone in front of friends, claiming that it's just a charity calling for a donation, when she knows that the voice on the other line will be someone from the bank or a bill collector.

Deniers who use this form of denial know exactly what they're doing and understand that it's wrong. They are also 100 percent aware of their LIB and the damage it's causing in the lives of others or to themselves. That's the main reason they resort to twisting the truth or lying to make the "facts" better suit their needs. Because of their awareness, they can't use denial to unconsciously ignore or reduce the severity of their LIB. Their only alternative, they believe, is to weave an interesting tapestry of lies to rewrite their actions—past, present, and future.

This type of denial may sound like the harshest of the six, but it's actually the easiest to treat because the denier is aware of the seriousness of his or her LIB. In addition, the longer these deniers continue to lie, the greater the sea of overwhelming evidence they create that others can present to them to prove that they are quite obviously in denial. Eventually, all of their lies and half-truths can be matched against the truth of what's really taking place in their lives. Such a confrontation leaves most deniers less resistant to doing something about their LIB, because once the facts finally come out, there really isn't anything left on the table for them to deny any longer.

If You Recognize That You've Been Denying by Lying . . .

Please stop feeling guilty. What usually comes with denial by lying is a sense of shame, low self-esteem, or anger with yourself for deceiving others. Despite these feelings you may have toward yourself, I have some great news: you may be using lies to make others believe that you're fine, but at least you're not oblivious to your situation. If this is you, then know that, compared to other deniers, you have the greatest chance of breaking out of your denial and changing your life for the better.

You should be thrilled to know that the first step deniers have to take in order to recover from almost any LIB is to recognize that they have a problem. Regardless of what your LIB is—drinking, drugs, financial woes, obsessive-compulsiveness, depression, physical or mental illness, a phobia—you have already completed the hardest step.

6

How Denial Hurts
More Than It Helps

Sometimes a little denial isn't necessarily a bad thing.

Picture this: You're in a car accident that leaves you paralyzed from the waist down. What would you say to a doctor who told you that you would never walk again? Would you accept his opinion and remain crippled for the rest of your life, or would you place yourself in immediate denial and prove your doctor wrong by doing what it takes to walk again one day?

Or how about this scenario: You're a happily married woman with three children when suddenly your husband leaves you for a lover. Emotionally, you're destroyed inside and terribly frightened about making ends meet. Would you show that fear around your children? Or would you block it out, put on a brave face, and ignore your own pain for the sake of your children?

There are many people who have beaten the odds, despite what others told them, by staying in denial about their situation. There are also plenty of people who have persevered through tumultuous events and circumstances by staying in some type of denial long enough to get themselves back on track—usually for the benefit of others. Instead of quitting, denial gave them a new sense of faith and allowed them to say things such as

"Yes, I can't walk, but I will walk one day."

"Yes, I wasn't born rich, but I will be successful."

"Yes, I made mistakes in my past, but I will live a better life."

"Yes, I'm starting at the bottom, but I plan on reaching the top."

Examples like these can make it difficult to accept that denial is all bad. But despite denial's ability to help you sometimes find the faith to overcome painful or hopeless situations, it's still a dangerous seed that, if left alone, can grow into something far more toxic than whatever it's trying to shield you from.

Knowing how and when a little denial can come to your rescue—and what can happen when it overstays its welcome—may help you understand your LIB a bit better. It can also help you finally discover what it is.

WHEN DENIAL IS HEALTHY (SORT OF . . .)

Sometimes life deals a surprise blow out of nowhere that can be impossible to accept right away without losing your composure, sanity, or hope. Immediately after experiencing a traumatic or stressful event or facing news you never expected or wanted to hear, you may need several days or weeks to fully process this unexpected event that's left you in a state of shock.

Whether it's experiencing an unforeseen death, being hit with divorce papers after fifteen years of marriage, living through the perils of war, being told you'll never amount to anything, getting passed up for that big promotion, or just staring into the mirror and realizing you're not getting any younger, there are times when facing reality may leave you unable to function. That's when a little denial can sometimes be a temporary lifesaver.

The shock of a traumatic event or a sudden problem can throw the mind into a condition that makes it impossible to think clearly and rationally. Being in denial can not only give you time to come to grips with the challenges that lie ahead but grant you the strength to persevere and accomplish things that are important to do at that moment.

An Unexpected Death

According to the most recent data from the National Center for Health Statistics (NCHS), about 2,448,000 people died in the United States in 2005. With a number that high, it stands to reason that most of us will live to see a few people we care for pass on. When someone dies from a disease or longtime condition, you may have time to prepare for the impending loss. But the death of someone we love is something that most of us are never ready for, especially when it comes by complete surprise.

For example, of those 2,448,000 deaths, 173,753 were injury-related, 33,541 were drug-related, 32,637 were by suicide, 21,634 were alcohol-related, 18,124 were due to assault, and 623 were due to pregnancy complications. According to the same statistical data compiled by the NCHS, 28,440 children under age one died as well. These types of unexpected deaths—as well as health problems that can result in sudden death, such as heart failure—leave millions of people each year grieving.

A brief period of denial can help you cope with such a loss so that you can take care of necessary and immediate tasks. Some people may feel guilty for being able to "shut out" their pain, but shutting out emotional pain temporarily for the sake of others can be a helpful coping mechanism that does more good than harm. For example, a widowed mother blocks her hurt to be strong for her children, or an adult son minimizes his grief for his deceased father so that he can comfort his widowed mother and handle the funeral arrangements.

Once your initial reason for using denial is finished, however, it's important to address your own pain and sadness by talking with someone and expressing your feelings. Generally, you should "be strong for others" only for as short a period of time as possible. If you keep yourself in denial too long and never deal with your own pain and sadness, your feelings can get tucked away and forgotten—or so you think. The truth is that not releasing your feelings creates an emptiness inside—and makes it that much more likely that you'll reach for a LIB to fill the void.

A Separation (or Any Relationship Breakup)

Most serious relationships reach a level where one or both partners place a tremendous amount of trust in the other and regard their partner as the most important person in their life. That's why any separation—whether a divorce or a breakup, and regardless of how much time has been invested in the relationship—can be traumatic enough to lead to instant denial.

For many deniers, separation can be even more painful to handle than a death. The person who caused them pain or sadness is not only still alive, but out there somewhere, keeping them stuck in denial with their hopes and their pain a lot longer than they should be. For brokenhearted individuals who believe that they can't live, succeed, or simply go on without that special person in their life, it may be healthier to temporarily imagine that their shattered relationship will mend at some point down the road. Or if one partner's inadequacies were the cause of the breakup, it can be far less painful for that person to deny any responsibility—and place it on the other person instead—in order to preserve self-esteem in the short term.

Sometimes we turn to denial not just for emotional reasons but for other interpersonal reasons. It may be more thoughtful to say that you're "taking time off" from a relationship or "trying a trial separation" to help others who are affected by the split-up, such as children or family. It may be smarter to ignore your broken heart in the short term in order to stay focused on your job so that you don't fall behind on your bills and responsibilities or seem weaker to your superiors or co-workers. Being in denial enough to believe that you might be able to rekindle a broken relationship may even prevent you from impulsively jumping into another unhealthy relationship too soon.

It's still important, however, to break out of denial as quickly as possible once you have a better handle on your self-esteem. I've watched some people stay in denial even when the ink is dry on the divorce papers and the ex-spouse has moved on and entered a new relationship. As I watched one woman I know let herself stay in denial to spare her heart, I saw it backfire in several ways: It caused her to repeat the heartbreak process over and over again each time she approached her ex and realized her love was unrequited. It also kept her believing that she wasn't back on the market. When other men floated into her life—potential mates who were far more emotionally healthy for her than her ex-husband—she dismissed them before giving them a chance. Denial not only placed her in situations where she continued to be hurt but kept her from finding a stronger, healthier relationship.

Recovering from Illness or Injury

It seems that every day you can pick up a paper, turn on the TV, or read a magazine or book and learn about someone who overcame the odds of recovery from a major illness or injury. For some people, being told by a doctor that they'll never be able to do something again—whether it's walking, seeing, hearing, healing properly, or living for more than a certain amount of time—can be tragic news. But, for some, such news sparks a desire to prove the medical community wrong. They use denial to ignore the odds, and they look at getting better as a challenge they plan to meet.

Turning to denial has helped many lucky patients find the faith to accomplish what their doctors thought impossible by enabling them not to give up. I'm a big believer in using denial for this purpose, so long as you're not denying the problem you're attempting to overcome. I've watched some people slip into complete denial that they even have the illness or injury in the first place, claiming instead that they've been misdiagnosed. That type of denial is extremely unhealthy, since it can prevent you from seeking the medical attention necessary to beat the odds.

For example, there are two ways of using denial for a person who finds out that he has cancer and is told that there is no cure and he has only six months to live:

- When denial is *healthy:* He denies that he'll survive for only six months and then forges ahead to do everything possible to prove the doctors wrong.

- When denial is *unhealthy:* He denies that he's even sick, despite what the doctors have told him, and decides to ignore the situation instead of facing it.

The difference between the two reactions is that those who use denial in a positive way embrace their situation and handle it in a healthy manner. They don't deny the facts—they just deny the hopelessness of the facts.

Confronting an Immediate Traumatic Situation

Ask combat soldiers who have seen their fair share of war if they ever stopped to mourn during battle, and you would be hard-pressed to find any who say yes. That's because if they did, odds are that they wouldn't be around to talk about it now. Although I was in the Air Force for under two years, I understand the discipline it takes to prepare for battle. Whenever I speak to soldiers and veterans who have served in wartime, I hear about that mental shift that has to take place in order to keep yourself focused, alert, and, most important, alive.

The traumatic situation doesn't have to be war. Any sudden, life-threatening situation—getting attacked, being in a bad fire or horrible car accident, finding yourself caught in the middle of an earthquake, flood, tornado, or other natural or man-made disaster—can make your brain slide into denial of your immediate losses so that you have the focus necessary to handle the situation, or escape it.

In these traumatizing situations, a little denial may save your life. If you can't pop yourself out of denial after the danger has passed, however, that's when it becomes unhealthy.

I once spoke with someone who had invited a person into his home who attacked him, robbed him, and left him for dead. After spending a month in intensive care, he was discharged from the hospital but found that he was unable to go back home. He kept the house he was attacked in but moved away and lived somewhere else for an entire year. He never addressed his fear of being attacked a second time but chose to stay in denial and pay for two places. Once the attacker was finally caught, he began to tear down the wall of denial he had built around himself for so long.

In most of these cases, the problem changes from being in denial about what you've lost to being in denial that your loss has affected you psychologically. That's when talking with a friend or even seeking a professional counselor may be necessary to get you to confront your loss, address its effect on you, and begin to grieve in a healthy way.

Handling Rejection

Receiving a blow to your self-esteem can come from many directions: from your friends, from your family, from your job, or from anyplace in life where you may not measure up to someone else's expectations.

Maybe you were overlooked for a big promotion, or you didn't land a job that everyone was certain you would be a shoo-in for. Or perhaps you approached someone you were attracted to, then got shot down because that person thought you weren't attractive, smart, or funny enough. Or maybe you're a child who, despite how hard you've tried, has never felt truly loved or respected by one of your parents. The more people we come in contact with in life and the more risks we take, the more likely we are to come across rejection at some point. Take rejection hard, and it can easily damage your self-esteem and undermine your confidence. Let it roll off your back, and it gives you the power to feel fine about yourself so you can push on, try again another day, and never give up.

One way people sometimes handle rejection with a tiny bit of denial is to spin the blame onto the person who rejected them. It may be healthier for a short period of time to imagine that your boss wasn't smart enough to see you for all you're worth, instead of admitting the truth that you have very little to bring to the company's table. It may be better to believe that the person who just turned you down for a date is pretentious and picky, instead of looking inward to see that maybe you're the one who really isn't much of a catch at the moment.

Another way to use denial is to put the blame on some unseen outside interference, which is typically something that's hard to validate. For example, one addict I worked with chronically blamed every single negative thing that happened in his life on every possible factor but himself. He found it better to believe that he never got into Princeton because his application was lost in the mail. To him it was easier to accept that he couldn't move up the corporate ladder at his job because other employees used unfair tactics or kissed up to the boss, even though he had no evidence to back up his theory. He had pointed a finger of blame at hundreds of people, things, and situations to excuse his shortcomings instead of pointing the finger at the one real problem—himself.

No matter how you use denial with rejection, it can spare your feelings when taking that initial blow to your ego. After all, not slipping into denial and instead absorbing the truth immediately could cause you to feel so down on yourself that you might think there's no point in trying again or in trying any harder than you already have. Usually it takes time, effort, and a lot of patience to accomplish any goal—especially one that you value enough to be hurt when you don't attain it. Not using denial to boost your spirits could lead you to quit on yourself too soon and sabotage your chances of eventually achieving what you want the most.

Denial can become unhealthy when it prevents you from at least looking at things from another perspective after the initial sting of rejection is over. Being rejected can be a great developmental tool because it can make you aware of certain changes you may need to make in order to grow—such as working harder, obtaining a new degree, building up your people skills, or improving your appearance or your health. If you allow yourself to linger in denial for too long, instead of asking yourself, "Was that the real reason I was rejected, or could I have done something differently?" you miss out on a chance to address potentially serious personal issues and thus reduce your risk of getting rejected in the future.

It's easy to get stuck in denial when you use it to recover from rejection, however, because it's such an ego booster, especially when other people agree with you simply to spare your feelings. But let's face it: no one likes to tell people they care about that they weren't the best person for the job or that they weren't someone's type because they obviously weren't attractive enough. The people you love and who love you often worry that they might crush your feelings with the truth. So instead of helping you grow with the truth, they end up agreeing with you in your denial.

The support of those around you may make you feel better about yourself; but, once you spring out of denial, it's important to let them know that you're now trying to use the rejection to make improvements to yourself. They may lie and tell you that you're perfect just the way you are—God love them—but at least you'll be making them aware of your plan. That way, the door will be open to them to offer insights that may help your improvement efforts.

Getting Older

If you're at this point in the book, you're already a few hours, days, or weeks older (depending on how fast a reader you are) than when you started. Aging is inevitable for everyone, but it leaves some of us— maybe even you—feeling depressed, unattractive, and incapable of doing the things we once did when we were young.

Being in a little denial about your age can be healthy when you don't take it too far. You've heard the expression "you're never too old to learn," right? Well, I believe you're never too old to do anything— so long as you never try to push yourself beyond your means. Throwing yourself into situations that may be way past your years might have negative consequences for your health, your relationships, or your career.

For example, thinking you can still bench-press three hundred pounds when you haven't lifted in decades could land you in the hospital, while deciding to wear that miniskirt you've had packed away for thirty years could make you the talk of the town—and not in a good way. It is always a healthy use of denial to deny your own maturity just enough to feel and act young at heart—but never in a way that can lead to injury or embarrassment. Here's the best rule of thumb to keep you from going too deep into denial: never try to look or act younger than you really are. Instead, try to look and act the best you can for your age, no matter what it is.

Taking the Risks That Can Change Your Life

Unfortunately, in most cases our brains use denial to cover up a problem that needs to be seriously addressed. The brain also can sometimes play an important role in keeping us in denial of certain facts and truths so that we're more likely to try new things when the odds aren't stacked in our favor.

Thinking about or being afraid of all the bad things that could happen in your life can leave you feeling too anxious, nervous, or depressed to enjoy what life actually offers you. This kind of thinking also can prevent you from trying things that would enrich your life— such as scuba diving, going on a hot-air balloon ride, or traveling overseas—simply because they seem risky. That's when using a bit of denial to help you avoid focusing too much on the what-ifs of life can let you take risks that would enrich your life immensely. Denial under these circumstances becomes unhealthy only when the denier gets too reckless.

Denial may also be healthy when it's used to stay diligent in pursuing your dreams. Countless people—both famous and ordinary— use denial to help them ignore the fact that they might not be good enough, rich enough, graceful enough, strong enough, fast enough, smart enough, or attractive enough to achieve their dream. As a way of facing the reality of their situation and the incredibly high odds against them, they use denial to protect themselves from the facts so they can persevere and succeed, in spite of those who believe they can't. Instead of failure, all they see is faith.

Unfortunately, nearly all of us eventually lose our faith and give up on our dreams—either because we've taken too long to achieve them or because they never seemed to begin to flourish. Coincidentally, that's one of the reasons nearly all of us are out of balance in the first place.

Part 2

Breaking Down the Wall of Denial

7

The Ten Questions
That Reveal Denial

We need to recognize a problem in order to solve it. That's what makes denial so toxic in our lives. After all, we can't fix what our mind never allows us to see.

The key to beating addictions such as drug use, alcoholism, and many other life-threatening LIBs is recognizing and accepting the problem. Nearly every expert in the field agrees that the moment addicts realize (1) they have a problem, and (2) they accept what that problem is, that step brings them 80 percent closer to beating the problem. Mind you, that doesn't mean that traveling the last 20 percent of the road to recovery is ever easy, but accepting their LIB means that they've already overcome the biggest obstacle to beating any addiction—breaking down their wall of denial.

The same can be said for conquering any other kind of LIB you may have. Once you acknowledge that, for instance, you work too much, spend unhealthy amounts of time on the computer, have a doomed relationship, or feel addicted to your BlackBerry, and then accept that this behavior is a problem that's hurting your life, true recovery can begin. It's awareness that starts you on the path to getting the appropriate help—whether that's using the lessons in this book or turning to a professional for guidance. Believe it or not, you've already taken the first step in doing exactly that. In fact, you began to break down the wall of denial after reading the very first page of this book.

Do you remember these questions?

1. Do you often feel depressed, angry, or anxious for no reason?

2. Have any of your friends, family members, co-workers, or anyone else close to you shown any concern about you recently—even if for no reason at all?

3. Do you spend a lot of your time judging other people?

4. Are you falling behind in any important areas of your life— work, family time, personal life?

5. Do you find yourself avoiding some situations (events, parties, special occasions) because certain people will be present?

6. Do you find yourself wanting and needing to be the center of attention?

7. Do you feel your life will get better or easier if a specific thing happens?

8. Do you tend to sweat the small stuff?

9. Do you constantly second-guess yourself after making decisions?

10. Have you noticed a decline in your health or appearance?

Your answers to these ten questions from the start of the book are one way of helping you discover where denial may exist in your life. That's why I presented them to you before teaching you exactly what denial is and how you may be using it to hide your LIB. These general questions were never meant to trick you, but simply to open your eyes to the fact that there may be some imbalances in your life right now that are the direct result of a LIB. Whether you said yes to just one or all ten of these questions depends on the severity of your LIB. But if you said yes to even one of them, you're definitely in denial about something—even if you still fail to see what that might be at the moment.

The reason I had you write your answers down on a separate sheet of paper and not in this book is simple. These ten questions aren't just the key for spotting denial in your life right now; they are also a tool you can use to spot denial down the road whenever it tries to creep back into your life—and trust me, it will. Turning to these questions every month—or whenever you feel a need to assess yourself—can help you find clues to what you may be in denial of—if you always answer them truthfully and honestly.

Here's why each of these questions is so important when it comes to spotting the denial you may have in your life.

1. DO YOU OFTEN FEEL DEPRESSED, ANGRY, OR ANXIOUS FOR NO REASON?

I don't care who you are or what you've accomplished in life—the fact is that none of us are ever perfectly happy all of the time. Even when your life is as close to perfectly balanced as it's ever been before, there are always going to be ups and downs now and then. Depression, anger, and anxiety are normal responses that we all experience from time to time. But when these three emotions become routine—either separately or collectively—it's a sure bet that you're in denial about something in your life.

When you consistently feel depressed, angry, or anxious, one or more of these reasons may explain it:

- A medical or neurological condition may be causing you to experience these emotions more often.

- It may be that you have not addressed a traumatic situation that happened in your past.

- You may have a problematic or stressful situation going on in your life.

- Something you expect to happen in your life sometime soon may be evoking these emotions.

Regardless of which of these reasons may explain your feelings, having any of these feelings chronically coming to the surface means there's definitely something out of balance about your life. However, it is possible to answer no to this question and still be in denial.

Most deniers feel extremely happy, contented, and relaxed when using their LIB. It's only when they don't use it that they experience extreme depression, anger, or anxiety. If you're a denier who uses your LIB all the time, it's quite possible that you feel ecstatic all the time. Some deniers fall into this trap. Their LIB makes them think their life is perfect, so they continue using it to keep their life perfect 24/7. For example, a drug addict might keep herself perpetually high so that she feels elated all day long, but deep down those three emotions are still there. They're just never allowed to show themselves as often as they would normally appear.

2. HAVE YOUR FRIENDS, FAMILY MEMBERS, CO-WORKERS, OR ANYONE ELSE CLOSE TO YOU SHOWN CONCERN ABOUT YOU RECENTLY—EVEN IF FOR NO REASON AT ALL?

You may have answered no to the first question, depending on how deeply in denial you are about the direction your life is going, but it's much harder to escape the watchful eyes of those who care about you. For me, it was those watchful eyes that pulled me out of denial's despair at the age of twenty-six. I was all three emotional states back then—depressed, anxious, and angry—but those were feelings I had managed to accept to the point of ignoring them. All around me, however, I could sense the constant concern of my friends, family, and eventually my ex-boss, who held the intervention that saved my life. I knew there were people who cared about me—and who just wished I could feel the same way about myself as they did.

When your life is in true balance, the people around you may be genuinely happy for you or they may envy the idyllic life you're living, but they rarely show a growing distress about your actions. When your life falls out of balance, those around you—especially those who truly care for you—tend to be less jealous and more nervous about the new direction in which your life seems to be heading.

Even if you honestly have no clue why others seem concerned about you, having people approach you with their concern is a clear sign that you're in denial about a LIB, especially if they are people who are dear to your heart and people you respect and trust. Deniers always have someone close to them—a family member, a co-worker, a close friend—who has reached out and tried to address the denier's specific issue. Sometimes that concern is expressed indirectly, such as happens when people stop by unannounced to "check in on you" or "just see how you're feeling." Any extra attention you're receiving that seems undeserved is typically done to make sure you aren't suffering from your LIB, even if your LIB is never brought up or discussed.

Another clear sign that you're in denial is finding yourself frequently annoyed with all of the attention coming your way. Those in denial unconsciously know why they are the center of attention and choose to interpret all the concern in a negative way. That can leave them feeling far more annoyed than flattered by the constant attention.

3. DO YOU SPEND A LOT OF YOUR TIME JUDGING OTHER PEOPLE?

Being constantly critical of the actions of those around you may not seem like a clear sign of denial, but it really is. It's an unconscious defense mechanism: you criticize others before they can criticize you for your LIB.

By being chronically hypercritical and judgmental of others, what you're doing, without realizing it, is bringing them down in a way that leaves you feeling superior to them; their opinions are thus devalued and seem less important than your own. That way, if and when anyone around you comes forward with concerns about your actions—or tries to speak to others about the mistakes they think you're making with your life—their opinion seems less valid to you, and more than likely false. You unconsciously convince yourself that those who are trying to help you aren't as smart or as caring as they appear, so it's much easier to dismiss their heartfelt concerns for you later.

Belittling others also places you in a position where you always feel you know more than those offering their opinions and concerns. Sometimes putting yourself in this position boosts your self-esteem, which only feeds your denial. You may find yourself saying or thinking things about your accusers like "they're just jealous," or "they don't understand my life," or "this is who I am, so they'll just have to deal with it." If you find yourself aiming any of these three thoughts at anyone in your life who seems to be worried about your actions, it's a sure sign that you're the one whose actions deserve to be judged instead.

4. ARE YOU FALLING BEHIND IN ANY IMPORTANT AREAS OF YOUR LIFE—WORK, FAMILY TIME, PERSONAL LIFE?

Ask yourself these questions:

- Am I as successful in my career as I should be, or have I taken a slow, or even sharp, decline in productivity?

- Is my relationship with my family stronger, or is it more strained with certain members of my family?

- Do I have as many friends as I've always had, or have I lost some along the way for some reason?

- Am I as fit as I want to be, or need to be for health reasons?

It's the basic rule of cause and effect: when you're in denial, your life is out of balance, and when your life is out of balance, it's because you're spending too much time engaged in some type of LIB that's leaving you less time to focus on the important aspects of your life and health. The less time you devote to these important aspects of life—your job, your family, your health, your mental well-being, your passions and dreams, your relationships with those around you—the more likely it is that they'll slowly begin to deteriorate or simply disappear.

It's hard to ignore when a major area of your life—not to mention several areas, or even every area—seems to be taking a downward turn. Granted, we don't always continue to succeed in our jobs, stay in perfect health, achieve every goal, boost our friendship base, and consistently get along with our families. Problems that can change facets of our lives for the worst—either temporarily or permanently—arise when we least expect them and may have nothing to do with a LIB or ourselves. But seeing any noticeable decline in a major area of your life could be a clear indicator of a denial problem.

Another telltale sign is how much effort you're putting into trying to repair what's damaged in your life. If something in your life that you care about is falling apart, the natural response is to try to fix it by asking for help, looking for the reasons why things aren't the way they once were, and beginning to take action to repair what's broken and make it better. Deniers don't do any of these things, however, because these actions would force them to face their LIB.

Instead, they simply accept the change for the worse in their life and move on. They accept that they have a harder time walking up a flight of steps, instead of placing the blame on being overweight. They accept that they can't afford to move out of their parents' basement, rather than tackle their credit problems and overwhelming debt. When someone close to them slips away from their life, seemingly for no reason, they simply accept the loss. They may try to ease the severity of that loss by saying things such as, "She never really loved me anyway," or "We just drifted apart," when the opposite is actually true. It's simply far easier—and safer—for deniers to push someone or something of value away—their health, their friends, their independence—than pull in the tools necessary to address what they are denying.

5. DO YOU FIND YOURSELF AVOIDING SOME SITUATIONS (EVENTS, PARTIES, SPECIAL OCCASIONS) BECAUSE CERTAIN PEOPLE WILL BE PRESENT?

Somewhere down the road, deniers end up leaving behind their fair share of casualties—a series of people who have long grown tired of trying to help them and have since given up. But a lot of deniers still have a few good people in their lives who haven't given up the fight to help them. These are people who aren't afraid to speak their minds, who tell it like it is, and who call the deniers on their actions whenever they see them using their LIB.

Deniers fear those who may confront them and those who can see through them, and so they tend to avoid these people at all costs. That's why those in denial often cancel at the last minute on others, break promises, or call ahead to get a rundown on who's attending an event before they make any commitment to go. A person in denial often tries to avoid an unpleasant situation by preventing any possible confrontation about their LIB from taking place, even if that means not showing up for an event they truly wish to attend.

It doesn't always work this way. Some deniers are fearless when it comes to going places where they might be called to account for their behaviors. Some people in deep denial have a high level of self-esteem that lets them feel in control of their life and tells them that they're choosing to avoid certain people for good reason. But how they act when speaking to these people they're otherwise trying to avoid can reveal how confident they truly feel inside.

Does this sound familiar? Then ask yourself, when you have a conversation with a person in your life you may be trying to avoid, do you

- Maintain eye contact, or do you feel the need to avert your gaze?

- Feel calm, or do you feel anxious, nervous, or upset for some unknown reason?

- Have an interest in what this person is saying, or do you worry about what he or she might say in relation to you?

- Enjoy the time you're spending with this person, or try to end the conversation as quickly as possible?

If you typically feel uncomfortable around someone, odds are that you already know why. There's something about yourself that you're afraid that person can see—something you're not proud of, something clouded by denial.

6. DO YOU FIND YOURSELF WANTING AND NEEDING TO BE THE CENTER OF ATTENTION?

You might think that deniers would want to avoid attention at all costs. After all, if everyone around them seems concerned about their life and their unhealthy behaviors, why would deniers want to stand out in the crowd and possibly attract even more concerns from those around them?

The truth is this: many deniers who suffer from aggressive or severe LIBs keep the spotlight directly on themselves as a defensive behavior to gain control over a situation. They feel that if they can dominate the situation, they are much more likely to be able to sidetrack others when necessary and shift attention far away from their LIB.

One reason they want attention may be to make others around them feel more uneasy and so less likely to bring up certain topics or to deal with the denier directly. I've seen some clients in interventions deflect attention away from their LIB by being the jokester, picking on people before they could fire off the first shot. Other clients have acted out in outlandish or unusual ways intended to repulse the family and friends at their intervention and make them eager to avoid the denier at all costs and be fearful about ever bringing up the LIB again. One addict I handled said the most hurtful and disgusting things to his mother, hoping his words would make her hate him to the point of giving up on him. But his denial didn't win that day, because I had already warned her that he might try that approach and explained why.

Another reason some deniers steal the spotlight may be, unconsciously, to try to make others around them feel as uncomfortable as they secretly feel. By doing and saying unusual or irrational things to draw attention to themselves, deniers essentially project their own discomfort onto others through their behaviors and actions.

7. DO YOU FEEL YOUR LIFE WILL GET BETTER OR EASIER IF A SPECIFIC THING HAPPENS?

Some deniers allow a LIB to linger and spin them out of balance because they simply don't believe it's a permanent part of their life. To give themselves some assurance that their LIB is temporary, they may do one of two things: they impose a deadline, sometimes event-related, that will magically transform their life and free them of their LIB without the slightest bit of effort, or they define what they feel would be the absolute breaking point or "final straw" that would signal the best time to finally take control of their actions. But until that moment arrives, they can blithely continue to use their LIB.

I've heard every final straw in the book:

"I'll stop working myself to the bone as soon as the baby is born."

"I'll finally get out of debt right after I land that senior management job."

"If I ever get a DUI, then I'll stop drinking."

"If I ever lose more than $1,000 on a bet, then I'll quit gambling."

"If I ever get busted and spend the night in jail, I'll stop using drugs."

"As soon as I get that bonus check, I'll go see a doctor about that strange tingling in my chest."

"If he ever hits me, then I'm leaving him for good."

Creating these imaginary deadlines or breaking points makes deniers feel that they have complete control over the situation and that their imbalance will definitely end at a certain time, by their hand. Unfortunately, that date never comes. What usually happens is that deniers eventually reach that deadline or hit that breaking point, but then never address their LIB. Instead, they downplay their actions, then begin conjuring up the next worst possible thing that could happen as a result of their LIB. Or they think of another specific event that will be their new deadline. Suddenly, the bar gets raised even further and the breaking point goes to the next level. I've watched as the same people who gave me those earlier excuses suddenly had new-and-improved excuses to throw at me, such as

"I'll stop being a workaholic when the baby can talk and needs me more."

"I'll get out of debt once I land that senior VP job."

"If I ever lose my license because of a DUI, then I'll stop drinking."

"If I ever lose more than $2,000 on a bet, then I'll quit gambling."

"If I ever go to jail for longer than a week, I'll stop using drugs."

"If I feel a tingling sensation anywhere else but my chest, I'll go see a doctor."

"I'll leave him if he ever hits my kids."

It's a vicious cycle that not only keeps you from ever getting out of denial but increases the risk of your actions becoming more and more hazardous to your life. As you continue to raise the bar, you find yourself more willing to place yourself in harm's way.

Another reason deniers love to establish a deadline or breaking point is that it allows them to admit they have a problem but to postpone getting help for it. Instead, by offering a definite date or breaking point that will make them bring their actions to an end or under control, they feel they can appease those around them who are concerned.

This tactic even eases a denier's guilty conscience. By setting the bar at something drastic—"if I get arrested," "if I lose my job," "if I blow a certain amount of money"—you can make yourself feel more at ease. So long as you never cross that line or breaking point, you feel as if your actions aren't as bad as those of others who share the same LIB.

These misconceptions can easily skew how dire your own situation really is. You may have your own perception of what a person with a "real" LIB looks like. I've worked with people who didn't think they were in debt because they hadn't lost their house yet, even though they owed money all around town. Another client of mine didn't feel like a hoarder because she didn't seem to have as much stuff in her house as someone she saw on *Oprah*. I've known doctors who didn't think they had a drug problem because they could still work, maintain their fancy cars, and never get busted. But the truth is, it doesn't matter where you set the bar on a LIB—if you aren't able to stop doing it, then it's a problem. Period.

8. DO YOU TEND TO SWEAT THE SMALL STUFF?

Let me ask you a few questions:

- Are you often told that you tend to lose your cool over things that others think are silly?

- Do your friends and family seem to tiptoe around you?

- Have you been called "critical" or "judgmental" on a regular basis?

Many deniers are typically on edge about every little thing because they worry that at any moment the secret they've been hiding from the rest of the world is going to be exposed. As a result, they become constantly edgy. The problem is that when others pick up on all that angst, deniers can't own up to why they're edgy without revealing that it's due to their LIB. That's why most deniers will shift the cause of their anxiety onto everything else. Sweating the small stuff helps cover up what's really making them nervous in the first place.

Finding problems with every little thing around you also creates a world of chaos that works like a smokescreen to hide your denial and your LIB not just from others but also from yourself. By placing so much unnecessary emphasis on all of the little annoyances in your life—or in the lives of others—you remain obsessed with putting out so many hundreds of tiny fires that there's never any time to turn around and notice the inferno your LIB is creating around you.

Being obsessed with trivial issues that don't seriously affect you or that aren't really a problem in the first place can even create what seems to some deniers like a reasonable opportunity to seek out and use their LIB—or at least to excuse their use of it. Using the ADAPT list, I can offer some examples:

- *Abuse:* Someone who is abusive amplifies the mistakes of others to have a reason to be more hostile toward them.

- *Disorders:* Someone with a phobia about traveling on the highway constantly finds fault with his vehicle as a reason to keep it in the garage—so he stays off the road.

- *Addiction:* I once worked with a girl who was in denial about abusing social drugs. To help create the opportunity to use these drugs, she would get all worked up over problems happening in her friends' lives so that she had an excuse to take them out and get high with them.

- *Physical issues:* A woman with poor hygiene blames others for rushing her and leaving her no time to freshen up properly.

- *The Truth:* Someone in denial about being greedy finds un-noticeable flaws in all her clothes as an excuse to purchase new clothes.

9. DO YOU CONSTANTLY SECOND-GUESS YOURSELF AFTER MAKING DECISIONS?

When you're in denial about something, no matter what it is, there's a part of you that unconsciously realizes that some of your decisions and choices may not be the wisest ones to make. This realization can create an inner conflict that causes you to feel less self-assured all-around, even about decisions and choices that have nothing to do with what you're in denial about. It's a strong uncertainty that can bleed into the confidence you bring to any action you may take.

Those in deep denial have a fear of making the wrong decision because they may not value their own opinion as strongly as someone else's. It can be something as insignificant as ordering a restaurant meal with your family, seeing what everyone else ordered when the plates arrive, and wishing you had ordered what someone else has. Or perhaps in driving someplace you've constantly second-guessed yourself at every point on the route where you have to pick between alternative ways of getting there. Some deniers are never able to feel good about what they decide on, especially if it's specifically for themselves. If you always question even the simplest decisions, then attack yourself for making a wrong choice, that ever-present lack of comfort with your decisions can be a sure sign of denial.

Another reason those in deep denial are always questioning their own actions is that they probably are used to having their actions constantly challenged by those around them. Some deniers have several people in their lives who always jump in and rescue them from the problems their LIB is creating. The presence of people like this in your life can make you less likely to trust your own actions for fear that something bad may happen without the assistance of others—whether the decision you're about to make is related to your LIB or not.

10. HAVE YOU NOTICED A DECLINE IN YOUR HEALTH OR APPEARANCE?

Do me a favor and step in front of a mirror. What do you see? Are you listening to what's being reflected back at you? Let me ask you these questions:

- Do you look tired most of the time?

- Do you seem to get sick a lot more often than your friends, family, or co-workers do?

- Have you put on or taken off a noticeable amount of weight?

- Do you often neglect to present yourself in the best possible way or in the way you used to present yourself?

- Do you not shower as often as you should, or do you consistently wear the same clothes several days in a row?

The point of these questions is this: do you look and feel the best you could, or is something preventing you from taking care of yourself? Mind you, I don't mean to say that a changed appearance is always a sign of something wrong. Time has a way of stealing away our youthful look, but regular exercise, eating right, and taking care of ourselves in other ways can hold back the hands of time. Being in

---

WHAT TO DO IF EVERY ANSWER IS NO

Is that you? If so, you're still not free and clear of denial just yet.

I've seen some individuals who were so deep in denial that it was possible for them to beat this quiz and answer no to every question. If you've also answered no to every question, that only means that your denial could be much stronger than the average person's. In the next few chapters, you'll be asked to map out your typical week and to call on others who know you best for guidance in revealing your LIB. If there's denial in you—and I suspect there is—the next few chapters will find it, even if this quiz wasn't an immediate success.

---

denial of a LIB, however, has a tendency to accelerate the aging process and leave us looking less like ourselves.

Because almost all severe LIBs are life-threatening, it's easy to see how having one would drastically change a person's appearance. Drug abuse, alcoholism, abuse, eating disorders, and most major physical and mental health issues can alter your appearance in ways that are almost impossible to hide. I witness physical change firsthand at every intervention I perform. When a family shows me pictures of their loved ones before their LIB interfered with their life, I'm always amazed at how different they look before and after. The change in one young girl in particular, whose LIB was using crystal meth, literally left me speechless. When I met with her family, I was told about how beautiful she used to be, and every picture they showed me certainly proved it. But on the day of her intervention the woman who walked through the door had aged twenty years in the space of just six months of drug abuse.

Many aggressive LIBs can be just as hazardous to your looks and well-being down the road, but even the most passive LIB can take its toll on your health and appearance, since any LIB regularly steals a substantial amount of time from your life. That's time you eventually have to make up by cutting back the amount of time you spend on other things. Unfortunately, the first thing usually affected is the time you spend on taking care of yourself. That's why noticing yourself slowly falling apart is an obvious sign that there's a LIB behind it.

8

Are You in True Balance?

I hope that answering and understanding the ten questions in chapter 7 has brought you face-to-face with your denial and, with any luck, a little closer to figuring out what your LIB might be. If you still haven't discovered what you're in denial of, however, it may be that looking at a week's worth of your day-to-day life can reveal it.

Having an imbalanced life means two things: One, there's something important either missing from it or not being received on a regular basis, such as love, self-esteem, security, or happiness. Two, something is being used to fill that void.

People turn to certain life-imbalancing behaviors, habits, and addictions to either fill the void or keep themselves blinded to what they're missing in the first place. One of the most effective ways to find your LIB is to throw your life on the scale—so to speak—to see which parts are heavier than others.

HOW ARE YOU SPENDING YOUR LIFE?

It's hard to deny a problem when the facts are placed right in front of you. The only way to find out if what you think is normal behavior is actually unusual, excessive, and ultimately imbalancing behavior is to break down your life and look at every single one of your actions in an average week. After you have your results, you can comb through them piece by piece to look for anything unhealthy that shouldn't be there. Once you see the tangible facts that reveal which areas of your life are out of balance, it becomes that much harder to stay in denial about the LIBs that are ruining your life.

That's where the seven-day denial audit can come to your rescue. What I'm going to ask you to do is take one week of your life and break it down minute by minute to look at not just everything you're doing in those seven days but everything you're feeling and thinking as well. I won't lie to you: measuring seven straight days of your actions, then recording exactly how you feel when doing them and what you're thinking about as you do them, is time-consuming. But then again, so is your LIB. The biggest difference between a seven-day denial audit and your LIB is that one can transform your life for the better and the other is the reason your life isn't what it could be. Believe me, seven days is nothing to sacrifice compared to the years your LIB has stolen from you up until now, not to mention the many years—and friends and opportunities—it plans to steal from you in the future.

Stepping back and finally dissecting the big picture—in this case, your life—is one of the greatest tools for breaking down the walls of denial. That you've come this far means that you're serious about doing something about the unhealthy things you already know about yourself, but the seven-day denial audit may help you learn even more. For most deniers, it's these undiscovered issues that make the biggest difference in turning around their lives.

I'm about to show you in a simple way just how out of balance your life is. The method may not always be perfect—but it's the perfect start.

THE SEVEN-DAY DENIAL AUDIT

When you step back and think about it, your life is really nothing more than a series of actions, thoughts, and feelings that you experience, either regularly or irregularly. How you divide up your life—week by week, day by day, hour by hour, minute by minute—says everything about who you are and ultimately decides everything about you. How you feel about yourself and others around you, what you accomplish in life, how healthy you are inside and out, how others perceive you—these are just a few of the factors you can control simply through your daily actions, thoughts, and feelings.

This is where the seven-day denial audit comes in. By breaking down each of your daily actions, it can become increasingly easy to see what you're doing wrong, what you're doing right, and what you're doing either too much or too little of in your life. For seven consecutive days, you'll track everything you do from the time you wake up until the time you fall asleep. Afterward, the end result should help you pick apart your day and find the actions that might be considered LIBs. By just adding up the amount of time you spend doing various things, you'll be able to see

- How long and how often you lean on your LIB

- What areas of your life may be suffering or diminished as a result of your LIB

- What factors may be triggering your LIB—what's making you feel a need to use it in the first place?

But the seven-day denial audit isn't just about tracking what you do with your time; it's also about understanding the "whys" and "whats" behind your actions. It's not just what you do that matters—it's why you do certain things and what you're thinking and feeling when you do them. Without that insight, it would be easy for you to change your red flags to another color without realizing it.

One of the best examples of this that I've ever witnessed was someone I worked with a few years ago. He was proud when he wrote down on his chart that one day after work he surfed the Web for a few minutes, then called a friend, then watched TV for a few hours with his children after dinner. After getting his family all settled, he then went to bed, where it took him about thirty minutes to fall asleep. That certainly sounds like a balanced life, doesn't it? But what if a few more details were added?

What I discovered was that he actually spent those few minutes of Web surfing on looking up sports stats—stats he hoped would predict the winning team for the big game that night. It turned out that the friend he called was his bookie; he made the call to place a sizable bet. And those three hours he spent watching TV with his kids? Not exactly quality time. Those were three frustrated hours he spent watching a game in which he lost a large sum of money. Finally, he couldn't fall asleep because he was worried how he was going to explain to his wife where his paycheck went. My understanding changed drastically when I was aware of the "whys" and "whats" behind his actions, as well as what he was thinking and feeling at the time.

Only looking at your actions can sometimes keep you stuck in denial, especially if your actions are perceived by others as productive and positive or don't seem to be habitual or excessive in any way, shape, or form. However, there may be reasons attached to some of your actions that make them unhealthy and imbalancing. That's why keeping track of not just what your body is doing but what's going on in your mind and soul as well is the only way to determine accurately if your actions are truly as healthy as they seem.

That's why I'm going to ask you to be specific about six factors when it comes to everything you do. All week long I want you to keep track of

- *Your time:* Write down how long (to the minute) you spend doing each specific activity.

- *Your body:* Write down what you are physically doing within that time.

- *Your mind:* Write down exactly what or whom you're thinking about within that time.

- *Your soul:* Write down how you honestly feel emotionally within that time.

- *Your stress:* Rank your stress level from 1 to 5, 5 being the highest.

- *Your conscience:* Pick one of these three words to describe how you feel about your action within that time: shameful, indifferent, or proud.

SAMPLE DAILY DENIAL AUDIT SHEET

You can either make your own daily denial audit sheets, using the steps I'm about to show you, or you can simply copy the following sheet and use it to keep track—minute by minute—of an average day of your life. You can also go to my recovery Web page, www .interventionnetwork.ning.com/, and download the forms for free. Note: if you're being thorough enough—and I want you to be— you'll need several sheets for each day.

DENIAL AUDIT SHEETS

DENIAL DAY #
DATE:

TIME	BODY	MIND	SOUL	STRESS LEVEL: 1=lowest, 5=highest	CONSCIENCE Shameful (S), Indifferent (I), or Proud (P)	CHECKBOX (use at end of week)
Start: Stop:				1 2 3 4 5	S I P	
Start: Stop:				1 2 3 4 5	S I P	
Start: Stop:				1 2 3 4 5	S I P	
Start: Stop:				1 2 3 4 5	S I P	
Start: Stop:				1 2 3 4 5	S I P	
Start: Stop:				1 2 3 4 5	S I P	
Start: Stop:				1 2 3 4 5	S I P	
Start: Stop:				1 2 3 4 5	S I P	
Start: Stop:				1 2 3 4 5	S I P	
Start: Stop:				1 2 3 4 5	S I P	
Start: Stop:				1 2 3 4 5	S I P	
Start: Stop:				1 2 3 4 5	S I P	
Start: Stop:				1 2 3 4 5	S I P	
Start: Stop:				1 2 3 4 5	S I P	
Start: Stop:				1 2 3 4 5	S I P	
Start: Stop:				1 2 3 4 5	S I P	

THE SIX THINGS TO WRITE DOWN FOR SEVEN DAYS

1. Audit Your Time

Certain LIBs are easy to spot by simply adding up how much time you're devoting to them. That's why it's important that, each time you make an entry, you write down the exact time (to the minute) you started an activity, then the exact time (to the minute) you stopped.

Ideally, there will be no time gaps between activities on your denial sheets—for example, if you finished a phone call with your mom at 6:37 p.m. and started doing the dishes afterward at 6:38, that's right on the money. Don't make a habit of having any gaps longer than a few minutes. A lot can happen in those few minutes—things that could be related to your LIB.

2. Audit Your Body

Next, write down the activity you're doing, no matter how trivial it is. Even if it's something you're doing for only two minutes of your day, I want you to write it down. If you're doing two things at once—watching TV while playing with your kids, for example—write down both activities, in order of importance. Here's the best rule of thumb: the only thing you don't need to write down is the time you spend writing on your denial audit sheets. Everything else—no matter how insignificant it may seem—is fair game.

3. Audit Your Mind

Sometimes it's not the activity that gives you clues to a possible LIB, but the thoughts that stir in your brain before or during the activity.

After you've written down an activity, ask yourself exactly what you've been thinking about while you were doing it, then write that down in just a few words. I've heard everything from "My wife" to

"My health," "How fat I am," "Nobody likes me," and "I hope I don't lose my home." Anything will do, even if it's just one word (such as "work" or "mother"); but, whatever you do, don't leave the space blank. I tell my clients that they are always thinking of something no matter what they are doing, so try to capture exactly what you're thinking during every activity.

4. Audit Your Soul

Next, write down exactly how you've felt emotionally during the activity in just one or two words. I don't want you to write down how you feel about the activity itself—just ask yourself what emotion you're feeling in general at that moment. Also, try to be as descriptive as possible. If you're not the best at expressing your feelings with words, try using any of the following words (which range in order of intensity) to start:

- Pleased, happy, ecstatic

- Upset, sad, depressed

- Nervous, anxious, petrified

- Annoyed, angry, furious

- Indifferent, unsympathetic

5. Audit Your Stress

Next, evaluate your stress level on a scale of 1 to 5, with 1 being the lowest and 5 being the highest. Again, I don't want you to write down how stressed you are about the activity itself, even though it may be the activity that's causing stress. Instead, I just want to know how stressed you feel in general at that moment. On the sample sheet that

I've provided and would encourage you to use, you can simply circle the number that best describes how stressed out you are.

6. Audit Your Conscience

Finally, I want you to describe how you feel about yourself for doing the activity with one of the following words: shameful, indifferent, or proud. Once again, on the sample sheet I've provided, you can simply circle S, I, or P; if you decide to make your own denial audit sheets, just write in the letter that describes your conscience during the activity.

If you find yourself choosing "indifferent" most of the time—if not all of the time—that's entirely fine and quite normal. But regardless of which letters end up filling your denial audit sheets, each has a lot to teach you about how in balance or out of balance your life is.

BEFORE YOU COUNT ONE SINGLE SECOND OF YOUR LIFE . . .

To get the most out of your seven-day denial audit, there are three rules to follow before even thinking about starting this LIB-revealing journey.

1. Pick an Average Week to Do Your Denial Audit

As anxious as I am for you to dive right into your denial audit, it's important to choose a week that you feel represents an average week in your life. Although it might be more convenient for you to try it while you're away on vacation or when you have some time off, you'll be robbing yourself of some of its eye-opening results. That's because most people tend to fall out of their usual behaviors when they take time off. I had one client who couldn't wait to get her life in balance, so she took time off from her job and gave her children to her ex-husband for the week. After seven days, her audit revealed no LIBs, but that result was unsurprising: her issues were centered on her job performance and her relationship with her kids. By planning a special week to take her audit, she had unconsciously eliminated any opportunity to highlight her LIBs.

So select a week you would consider a typical seven days for you. The more average the week you choose, the more information you'll pull from the audit experience.

2. Be as Specific as Possible About Every Single Minute

If you're at work from nine to five, I don't want to see "work" written all the way down your list. Why? Because no one truly works a full eight-hour day. During those eight hours you're being paid to work, you make trips to the coffee machine, you visit the bathroom, and you sneak in personal phone calls. You may spend time surfing the Web, texting, having conversations with co-workers, eating and drinking, or doing dozens of things that aren't related to your job. I want to know about every single experience—minute by minute—even if what you're writing down seems completely irrelevant.

In fact, many of the sort of activities I want you to write down may seem too innocuous to note, such as exercising, cleaning, brushing your teeth, or speaking with friends. I'm not expecting all of your activities to send up red flags the way some activities do—such as excessive drinking, gambling, doing drugs, or crying—and you shouldn't either. Just pay attention to every detail, thought, and emotion and then let the facts reveal what they may.

THE BEST TIME TOOLS

Here is a short list of items that can make your seven-day audit much simpler and more accurate.

A Stopwatch

To audit yourself thoroughly, you need to record how much time you spend on every single activity as precisely as possible. I recommend investing in a stopwatch or a digital watch with a stopwatch feature. Simply guessing or estimating how much time you spend on each action in your typical day makes it harder to spot and stop the behaviors that could lead to—or actually be—a LIB.

A Digital Recorder

Sometimes it's not easy to find the time to record information on your denial audit sheets or to keep them handy. To ensure that you get the most accurate breakdown of your week and to make recording information a more convenient and discreet process, it can be helpful to use a pocket digital recorder, or any other kind of recording device that makes it less difficult to keep track of your daily activities. If it works more efficiently for you, simply record yourself before and after each activity you perform throughout the day, then add the information from the recordings to your sheets each night.

A Day-Timer

You may have no problem writing down every detail of your day but feel somewhat self-conscious doing it around others. If you worry that other people may wonder why you're writing all the time, make reduced copies of the sample daily denial audit sheet and place them inside your Day-Timer. Each time you audit your activities, you'll innocently look like you're simply organizing your life.

3. Don't Lie to Yourself . . . About Yourself

The more honest you are with yourself when taking this audit, the more it will reveal about your life and the more power you'll have to restore balance to it. Your honesty that determine whether you create a denial audit that's guaranteed to make your life, and the lives of those who care about you, much healthier and happier. Before you start, and throughout the entire week, remember the following:

- If you're completely honest with yourself, you will find imbalances in your life.

- Know that everyone has imbalances and no one is perfect.

- Take comfort in knowing that all imbalances can be corrected or kept in check—either with this book or with the help of a specialist.

9

Analyzing Your Audit . . .
to Find Your Answers!

The week is over. Your seven days of auditing yourself are finally over. And right now you should have a slew of sheets to pore over and a lot of information that you're not quite sure what to do with.

Now the fun part begins—and I say "fun" because you've now reached the stage where most deniers finally connect with the life-imbalancing behaviors they've been turning to for years. I don't want you to be upset by what you find out in this chapter. Instead, I want you to be excited that you've taken another healthy and necessary step to tear apart the denial that's been protecting your toxic LIBs all this time. So, let's get started!

ANALYZING YOUR AUDIT—STEP-BY-STEP

Evaluating your denial sheets is something you're going to do in stages, since there are many different ways to use this information to find patterns that point to a LIB—or that could trigger your need to use one. I'll get into more detail later on how to do this and what to look for. For now, I'll simply spell out the seven ways in which you'll review your audit sheets:

- First, you will think about the *obvious* problems or issues that you noticed during the week simply by being more mindful of your actions.

- Second, you will tally up your *time* by adding up and examining how much time you spent doing each activity.

- Third, you will look at the *body* portion of the charts. After you look at all of your actions and activities, I'll help you determine which are healthy and which are not.

- Fourth, you will examine the *mind* portion of your audit to find out what you were thinking before, during, and after every activity.

- Fifth, you'll review the *soul* section of your charts to see what your moods were like before, during, and after each activity.

- Sixth, you will examine the *stress* section to see where your levels are, not only during each of your activities but in the moments before and after as well.

- Seventh, and finally, you'll take a look at the *conscience* portion of your audit sheets to see where you stand personally about how you spent your week.

1. Look for the Obvious

Sometimes when we're told simply to pay more attention to our own lives, certain things about ourselves that weren't obvious before suddenly become clear. So before you begin to analyze any of the facts and figures written down on your denial audit sheets, I want you to answer a few questions:

- Did you see something about yourself this week that you never noticed before and that concerns you?

- Were there certain activities, thoughts, or feelings that you felt nervous or embarrassed about writing on your sheets?

- Are there certain things you've written down that you would dread having anyone else—or someone in particular—read?

If you answer yes to any of these questions, chances are that a LIB was the reason. I want you to find those activities on your sheets that evoked this response from you and place an "O" next to them. (If you're using the sample denial audit sheets provided in the last chapter, place an "O" in the far right column labeled "Checkbox.")

2. Look at the Time

Next, run through your list of activities and add up exactly how much time you spent doing each of them on both a daily and weekly basis. Now step back, look at the numbers, and answer the following questions:

- Are you surprised at how much time you spent doing a certain activity?

- Are you amazed at how little time you devoted to other activities?

- Are there any activities besides sleeping and working on which you spent more than two hours a day on average?

Because you did your denial audit during an average week of your life, there should not have been any new activities that were gobbling up excessive amounts of time in your week. So if you've answered yes to any of these questions, that points to an obvious imbalance in how you're budgeting your time.

Place a "T" next to each activity on your denial sheets that seems to have taken up an excessive amount of time. If you've already put an "O" next to any of these activities, just put a "T" next to it.

But you're not through just yet! Sometimes it may not be obvious what's considered an appropriate amount of time, what borders on being excessive, or what's less than average. Before you move on to stage 3, take a look at the following list of basic activities to see how long each should generally take.

LIBs such as being addicted to shopping, cleaning, television, texting, eating, exercising, or working can be spotted fairly quickly when you compare your numbers to the national average for these common activities. LIBs such as being narcissistic or lazy can also be easy to notice when you see how others spend their free time.

See how you fare compared with these national daily averages compiled by the U.S. Department of Labor's Bureau of Labor Statistics. If you find that the total time you spend on any activity is either much greater or much less than the average time most people devote to it, then, again, place a "T" next to that activity on your sheets.

Activity	Subcategory	Average Hours Per Day		
		Total	Men	Women
Personal care		9.33	9.14	9.51
	Sleeping	8.57	8.52	8.60
	Grooming	.67	.54	.79
	Health-related self-care	.07	.05	.08
Eating and drinking		1.24	1.27	1.20
	Eating and drinking	1.11	1.13	1.09
	Travel related to eating and drinking	.12	.13	.11

		Average Hours Per Day		
Activity	**Subcategory**	**Total**	**Men**	**Women**
Household activities		1.84	1.43	2.22
	Housework	.64	.29	.97
	Food preparation and cleanup	.52	.28	.74
	Lawn and garden care	.21	.30	.12
	Household management	.14	.12	.16
	Interior maintenance, repair, and decoration	.08	.12	.05
	Exterior maintenance, repair, and decoration	.06	.09	.03
	Animals and pets	.09	.09	.10
	Vehicles	.04	.07	.01
	Appliances, tools, and toys	.02	.03	.01
	Travel related to household activities	.05	.05	.05
Purchasing goods and services		.78	.63	.92
	Consumer goods purchases	.39	.31	.48
Caring for and helping household members		.53	.33	.72
	Caring for and helping household children	.42	.25	.58
Caring for and helping non-household members		.20	.17	.23
Working and work-related activities		3.81	4.52	3.14
	Working	3.47	4.09	2.89
	Other income-generating activities	.03	.03	.02
	Travel related to work	.28	.36	.21
Educational activities		.43	.41	.44

Activity	Subcategory	Average Hours Per Day		
		Total	Men	Women
Organizational, civic, and religious activities		.35	.28	.41
Leisure and sports		5.11	5.48	4.76
	Socializing and communicating	.73	.67	.78
	Relaxing and leisure	3.70	4.02	3.40
	Watching TV (part of relaxing and leisure)	2.62	2.88	2.38
	Arts and entertainment (other than sports)	.09	.09	.10
Sports, exercise, and recreation		.35	.45	.25
	Participating in sports, exercise, and recreation	.32	.42	.22
	Attending sporting or recreational events	.03	.03	.03
Telephone calls, mail, and e-mail		.19	.13	.24
	Telephone calls (to or from)	.11	.06	.15
	Personal mail and messages	.02	.02	.03
	Personal e-mail and messages	.05	.05	.05

Source: U.S. Department of Labor, Bureau of Labor Statistics.

3. Look at Your Actions (Body)

Run through all of your sheets and look for any activities that could be a possible LIB. (You can use the lists in chapter 2 to remind yourself of the most common LIBs.) Obviously, if you're in denial about a LIB that involves clearly unhealthy activities—such as using drugs, being abusive, or gambling obsessively—your actions alone instantly reveal a misuse of time. But you may also find on those lists one or two activities that indirectly relate to a LIB. If you feel there's a strong enough connection with any activity, mark it with a "B."

Other activities may not be as obvious, especially if they are activities that seem harmless, are rewarded by society, or remain shielded by your denial. So for each activity you haven't already marked with a "B," ask yourself the following questions:

- Is this an activity that at least three people close to me have criticized or expressed their unhappiness that I'm engaged in it?

- Is this an activity that always seems to happen either when I feel stressed or directly afterward?

- Is this an activity that I don't let others know that I do or one I would be nervous to admit that I do?

- Is this an activity that I've criticized others for doing?

- Is this an activity that makes me anxious, angry, or depressed if I can't do it and happy or relaxed when I do engage in it?

- Is this an activity that, if someone asked me to stop doing it, I'd find it hard or impossible to give up?

Saying yes to one or two of these questions may not be a problem. For example, having sex could easily be an activity you would say yes to when answering the last two questions. But if you find yourself saying yes to three or more of these questions about any particular activity, it has the potential of being a LIB, so mark it with a "B."

4. Look at Your Thoughts (Mind)

Although a LIB usually makes us feel better by temporarily filling the void we have in ourselves, it's not always as effective at shutting down our thoughts. That's why what you're thinking isn't always in synch with what you're doing or feeling. If negative thoughts are attached to a specific activity, odds are that it's related to your LIB—or it *is* your LIB.

For example, here are just a few ways, taken from the ADAPT list, in which your thoughts may contradict your actions:

- *Abuse:* Hanging out at the library all night long may make you look studious, but not if the thoughts you're thinking while you're there are centered on figuring out how to stay longer in order to avoid someone who's abusing you at home.

- *Disorders:* Spending quality time with your children may look perfectly normal, but not if that's the only time you seem to have depressive thoughts.

- *Addiction:* Toiling away on an exercise bike may sound healthy, but not if you're obsessively thinking about how much you secretly hate your body and everyone else who's in shape.

- *Physical issues:* Keeping yourself busy all day may seem productive, but not if you're simply trying to distract yourself from worry about a health issue.

- *The Truth:* Having a girls' night out with your friends may seem sociable, but it's not healthy if all you can think about is how much you resent them for having everything you don't.

As you go through your sheets, search for any activities accompanied by negative thoughts (for example, bitter, self-loathing, depressive, selfish, manic, or anxious), then put an "M" next to them. Afterward, look at the activity directly above the one you've just marked. Did something happen beforehand that triggered your negative thoughts? Did you see something, do something, not do something, or hear something that may have spun your thoughts negatively afterward?

If so, don't put an "M" next to the activity associated with negative thoughts. It may simply be a normal, expected reaction, not a LIB. It could be that seeing your neighbor driving her new BMW made you think jealous thoughts while trimming your hedges. Maybe hearing an old love song made you sad as you remembered an old flame. However, I still want you to ask yourself why you had such a negative reaction, and whether you consider that reaction normal behavior. If your thoughts don't seem to match the thoughts that most people would have under the same circumstances—or your thoughts are ones you wouldn't dare share for some reason—they could be linked to a LIB.

5. Look at Your Emotions (Soul)

No one is happy 100 percent of the time, but looking more closely at activities that make you feel miserable can clue you in to a possible LIB. Certain negative emotions—such as anger, frustration, depression, anxiety, and fear—tend to be associated with a LIB. The tricky part is that certain positive emotions—such as love, happiness, and contentedness—can also be easily associated with a LIB.

When you suffer from certain aggressive or severe LIBs—such as drinking, gambling, sex addiction, or drug abuse—you can often feel the happiest you've ever felt when you're engaged in the LIB. It's only afterward—when the high from your LIB begins to wear off—that the negative feelings creep back into place.

Look for activities on your sheets associated with extreme changes in your emotions, either negatively or positively. If you come across an activity that made you feel an extremely negative emotion for a prolonged period of time—such as anger, anxiety, or depression—mark that activity with an "E."

If you come across an activity that made you extremely happy or calm, take a look at the emotions you felt prior to and then immediately after that activity. If you notice that you were angry, anxious, or depressed prior to that activity, happy or calm during the activity, and then had the same negative feelings after the activity, it might be LIB-related, though that's not always the case. For example, you might have felt angry after a bad day at work, felt happy while spending time with your kids, then felt angry again when you went back to dealing with work-related matters. However, if your LIB is alcohol, you might experience the same negative-positive-negative pattern when you're drinking.

That's why I want you to seriously examine these activities and ask yourself if they seem normal. If the activity is commonly considered a healthy activity that should make you happy and calm, such as doing yoga, reading a book, or spending time with friends and family, leave it unmarked. But if it strikes you as an activity that's not commonly known to make others feel good, then mark that activity with an "E."

6. Look at Your Stress Levels

All of the activities on your denial sheets should have a stress ranking between 1 and 5, with 5 being the highest. For now, I want you to look only at those that you've ranked a 4 or 5. Place an "S" next to each of these.

Any activity that makes you feel uncomfortable enough to earn a 4 or 5 on your stress meter is a clear-cut LIB. Some high-stress activities are unavoidable—for example, trying to make dinner while managing all four of your kids may make you want to pull your hair out, but it may be an inescapable task you absolutely have to do each day. It's still a LIB, however, because it's an activity that's obviously causing you to feel anxious, stressed, and out of balance, which is never healthy to experience on a regular basis.

Now look at the next activity directly below any activity you've marked with a 4 or 5. Did your stress levels drop down to 1 with that activity? If so, that activity could be a LIB. Stressful situations often trigger us to use a LIB immediately to calm ourselves down. Or it could be that the activity that scored a 4 or 5 was not in fact stressful at all. That score may have been simply a reflection of the pent-up stress that some deniers feel when they desperately need to use their LIB but can't right away.

Search through all of your activities and look for pairs where the first activity ranks a 4 or 5 and the activity immediately below it ranks a 1 or 2. If they feel related to each other in the ways I've just described, mark them with an "S" if they don't already have one. But be reasonable as you make this judgment. For example, if visiting your in-laws scores a 5 and finally leaving their house and driving away scores a 1, it's probably not a LIB—it's just life!

7. Look at Yourself

At one time or another, any one of us might not be the best judge of what's right and what's wrong. If we always knew the difference and acted accordingly, we wouldn't all be in denial about something, now would we?

But when you do something that's not the best choice for yourself, isn't there often something inside you that's not afraid to let you know? Call it your gut or your little inner voice, but if you often feel guilty when you spend more time doing what's wrong, you may feel equally guilty when you spend less time doing what's right. It's your guilt that can flush out a LIB that may have escaped every other measure. It's also your guilt that helps you see which areas of your life need more attention.

- *For every "S" you find:* Mark that activity with a "G." If it's an activity that already has several letters next to it, it's definitely related to your LIB—or it *is* your LIB. But if it's an activity that isn't marked with any letters yet (except for the one you're about to give it), it may not be a LIB at all. Some people—especially those who give of themselves—can feel guilty doing the things they should be doing for themselves, like taking a breather and taking care of themselves for a change.

- *For every "I" you find:* Don't write anything next to these activities. Finding all the activities you've marked with an "I" may take a while because odds are that you have a lot more of this letter on your sheets than any other letter. Having "I" all over your sheets is a mixed blessing—it means you're not doing anything you regret, but at the same time you're not doing anything that's helping to build your self-esteem. I'll show you later in the book how to turn an "I" into a "P," but until then, you can leave these activities unmarked.

- *For every "P" you find:* Check to see if activities marked with a "P" have any other letters next to them. If they have at least two other marks, mark that activity with a "G." Sometimes we can be proud of things we shouldn't be proud of, such as when an alcoholic takes pride in being able to handle her liquor, or a video game addict brags about his score on a certain game. Odds are that if you already have two or more letters next to an activity, it's a LIB, no matter how proud of it you may be.

However, if the activity has only one letter next to it, or none, circle it. It may be an activity I'll want you to try to incorporate more into your life down the road.

THE LETTERS THAT REVEAL YOUR LIB!

For most deniers, running a week of their life through all seven stages is enough of an awakening to finally see the LIBs they are relying on. If your eyes haven't already been opened to any of your own

LIBs, you should at least have a bunch of activities with letters written next to them. This exercise will help you define each one for what it really is.

First, find all of the activities with the most letters written next to them, starting with those that have seven letters, and pick one to start. Write down that activity on a sheet of paper, followed by the words "is an activity that. . . ." For example, if "work" is the activity on your sheets that has the most letters next to it, you would write on your paper: "Work is an activity that. . . ."

Next, look at the letters you wrote down next to that activity. You're about to write your own definition for it, using those letters as a guide. Each letter represents a part of a sentence.

O—"is something that troubles me."

T—"takes up too much of my time."

B—"isn't normal behavior."

M—"always seems to be centered on negative thoughts."

E—"always seems to be centered on negative emotions that I don't like to feel."

S—"leaves me stressed out or is triggered by stress."

G—"I know deep down, is wrong to do."

Now, I want you to add the phrase that each letter represents to the sentence you just started to write. For example, if one of the activities you've audited was drinking and you marked it with T, B, M, and G, then your realization is: "Drinking is an activity that takes up too much of my time, isn't normal behavior to do, always seems to be centered on negative thoughts, and I know deep down is wrong to do."

Congratulations! You've just defined how you feel about something you do in life. I want you to now read the sentence you've just written aloud to yourself and absorb how it makes you feel. Keep saying it aloud, and as you do, let me ask you,

- Does the statement sound similar to what others who care deeply about you have told you recently?

- Does it sound like the last words you heard from others whom you once cared about but either lost touch with or don't speak to now for some reason?

- Does it sound like something that makes you want to stop that activity?

If you say yes to any of these three questions, the activity you've just defined is a LIB. Now try the same exercise with the rest of the activities with the most letters next to them. Anything with between three and seven letters next to it isn't a behavior that's healthy for you and, as such, is contributing to pulling your life out of balance.

Is this system foolproof? Not always. As I'll show you in the next chapter, some LIBs aren't as easy to track using a denial audit. How useful this audit is to you also depends on just how honest you are with yourself when taking it. But there are a few ways in which you can enhance the audit experience to make sure it's not you that's still holding you back. Here are three strategies that may work for you.

Try to Get a Second—or Third—Opinion

It's usually much easier to see the imbalance in other people's lives than it is to see the imbalance in your own. If you're not aware of which numbers from your audit seem off, those closest to you may be able to point a finger at those activities that seem excessive or poor uses of your time. If you've pored over every second of your denial audit and still can't seem to find any discrepancies or patterns that point to a LIB, do yourself—and your life—a favor. Take a leap of faith and turn the audit over to someone you trust—someone who has nothing to gain by being dishonest with you.

Even if you feel you've already found one or two imbalances in your life on your own, asking someone in whom you have complete faith to evaluate your audit can play a major role in spotting even more imbalances even faster. What makes this step so valuable is that those we trust typically are well aware of our LIBs. Showing them your audit sheets and asking for their assistance lets them know that you mean business about taking charge of your life, which may give them the opportunity and the courage to finally address your LIBs with you.

If you don't have anyone you trust, try taking your sheets to an expert. If you suspect your LIB is health-related, make an appointment with your family doctor. For all other matters, consult a specialist. (You can find several resources to help you find someone in chapter 18.)

Do a Double Denial Audit

If you're seriously determined to find every possible LIB in your life, and if you have the means, try asking someone (or several people) you trust to monitor how you spend your week from their perspective—either simultaneously or during another average week. Obviously, there are certain things about you that can't be noticed by an observer—such as what you're thinking, what you're feeling, and what your conscience is telling you—but this person may be able to help you in other ways that you can't be objective enough to do yourself.

Because most of us never have someone around us 24/7, try dividing the job among different people—for example, your roommate or spouse in the morning, a co-worker during office hours, and your friends at night. If possible, try to pick people you'll be in the presence of but not necessarily in constant contact with, so they can observe you more from a distance. Then ask them to keep track of the following things:

- What you're doing (*body*)

- How long you're doing it for (*time*)

- What you're talking about when you're doing it, which may provide insight into what you're thinking or feeling (*mind* and *soul*)

- How stressed you seem when doing it (*stress*)

You may think that this technique would be less effective or even pointless. After all, if you know people are monitoring your actions every minute of the day, you'll be more likely to change what you're doing, right? That's exactly what I'm hoping for.

We tend to change our actions and behaviors in a more positive way when we feel we're being watched and judged. Therefore, you're more likely to rely less on your LIB, or you may find your life being more inconvenient during this week as you desperately look for even more covert ways to turn to your LIB. These are the moments you need to focus on. If you find yourself feeling guilty, being secretive, or changing your routine, whether slightly or drastically (or changing your routine from your first denial audit, if you're not taking one simultaneously), these are serious red flags that should help you lock down right away on what may be a LIB.

Another positive outcome of the analysis of others is the chance to see how you may be misinterpreting certain actions. For example, you may think you spent five quality hours of time with your kids one afternoon, when someone else may see that time as five hours spent surfing the Web as your kids played in the room next to you. Looking for such discrepancies can pinpoint a problem area that may hide a LIB.

Afraid to ask for this kind of help? If for some reason you feel awkward about revealing the fact that you're taking a denial audit, remember that everyone is in denial. That means that every single person you're asking to help you is in the same boat. You're just one step ahead of them by being honest with yourself that it's time to do something about it. In fact, you might even use your request for help as an opportunity to introduce them to the theories in this book. There's no greater gift you can give those you care about than the tools to make their life even better than it already is.

However, if you still find it awkward to admit what you're attempting to do, I find it's best to tell the people you're asking for help that you're looking for ways to manage your time better. Technically, that's not a lie at all, since a LIB is in essence a mismanagement of your time. And since everyone could always use a little improvement with time management, telling your prospective helpers that this is your goal may help you feel more relaxed and less self-conscious. Your helpers will simply think you're looking for a way to become more efficient, when in reality their observations will help you see your life from another perspective.

Audit Your Denial at Least Every Six Months

Once you've used a denial audit on yourself, found your LIB (hopefully), and sought help to treat it using the tools I'll be showing you later in this book, the good news is that you can return to the audit at any time afterward. Every audit after the first one will enable you to measure your progress. Successive audits can even give you some insight into any new LIBs you may be using, give guidance on touchier spots of your life that may require extra attention, or help you be more honest with yourself if you weren't as up-front when taking the first audit.

As important as the denial audit is as a way to flush out LIBs, I don't recommend doing it too often. Denial can be something that's easy to remove with the right tools, but it's also easy to let it slowly crawl back into your life. Doing a denial audit too soon after using the tools in this book might not reveal any immediate clue that your LIB is reemerging and instead leave you feeling like your life is permanently back on track. That kind of result can cause some deniers to believe they're completely free of denial, so they never bother to repeat the steps in this book and eventually fall back into denial. Instead, I'd recommend doing your denial audit once every six months—or even up to once a year—since most deniers who return to their LIB usually do so to some degree by that time.

I'll ask you to do what I have clients do: Pick one or two important or meaningful dates that you would never forget—a birthday, the anniversary of a celebration, or maybe something less celebratory such as the anniversary of the death of a loved one or of a loss caused by your LIB. It should be a date whose significance gives you strength or motivation. But don't start your next denial audit on that actual day. Most of us do things on important days that we might not do normally, since we might be in the presence of people we don't typically see and we may act more reserved. Instead, use the significant date you've chosen strictly as a reminder to start a seven-day denial audit the next day.

10

The Denial That Time Hides

Thanks to the seven-day denial audit, many readers of this book may have identified the LIB they've been hiding behind their denial. If you still haven't found yours, there may be three reasons why.

REASON 1: FLEXIBILITY

The first reason you may not have discovered your LIB is that certain LIBs are more flexible than others and can be rearranged. Depending on which LIB you have,

- It can be broken into smaller pieces

- It can be traded in for new ones

- It can be interchangeable with other LIBs

Some LIBs Can Be Broken into Smaller Pieces

It's often the case that a LIB is present but hard to spot because the denier has found a way to divide his or her actions into smaller, less noticeable, chunks of behavior.

For example, someone whose LIB is over-exercising may split his workouts into several routines that he performs at different times of the day, or even at different locations, so that others around him never get a chance to see that all of his workouts add up to an unhealthy amount of exercise. Or a person whose LIB is shopping obsessively might purchase only one or two items each day from a certain store, seeming perfectly in control, yet she may also be shopping online or over the phone. I treat a lot of alcoholics and drug addicts who like to use this technique. By spacing out their drinks or drug use through-out the day, they always seem in control because they never appear overly drunk, even though they're perpetually high, from sunup to sundown.

By dividing your LIB into smaller LIBs, you're more likely to see your actions fly under the radar, where they'll be missed by those around you—and even by yourself. Yet, collectively, these smaller LIBs could add up to a single LIB that's larger and a lot more life-damaging than it appears to be.

Some LIBs Can Be Traded In for New Ones

Some deniers may find themselves substituting one LIB for another. As soon as one LIB has run its course, they shift effortlessly into an-other type of LIB. The reasons for jumping to a new LIB can vary, depending on the denier. But typically this happens for one of two reasons.

The first possible reason is that the denier has used his or her LIB to its fullest extent and can't push it any further. When these deniers no longer get the same sense of fulfillment from their LIB, they immediately seek out another LIB to replace it. For example, I've handled many workaholics who stopped feeling as satisfied when they finally succeeded beyond their wildest dreams, or they retired, or for some reason they no longer had to struggle in their career. To chase that high again, they suddenly shifted their work drive into other areas of their lives, such as being overly involved in the lives of their kids.

The second possible reason is that the denier has found another LIB that is far more effective at filling the void in his or her life. Many of my clients who suffer from the severe LIB of addiction experience this effect. They find themselves leaping from addiction to addiction, searching for a more powerful high when they stop experiencing the same relief they once received from their prior addiction.

This is why addicts tend to get progressively worse and fall deeper into their addictions if they never receive treatment. The sense of fulfillment they used to achieve from a few drinks suddenly isn't enough to fill the void they feel inside. So they either use more of a substance to raise that level of fulfillment or turn to something stronger to recapture the sensation.

That's exactly what happened in my own life. My first LIB was abusing alcohol at fifteen, but as I got older I found myself chasing that next big high through other drugs. I went from drinking excessively to using black beauties, mescaline, cocaine, ecstasy, and finally, crystal meth. Eventually, no matter what I tried, I could never seem to achieve that same feeling of satisfaction that I once got from just alcohol, so I just kept chasing that high until it almost killed me.

Some LIBs Can Be Interchangeable with Other LIBs

Some deniers can flip-flop from one type of LIB to another and feel equally satisfied in filling the void they feel inside themselves. For instance, someone who's chronically depressed may use an assortment of LIBs to distract herself from her sadness, ranging from drug use to eating disorders, risky sexual practices, and other LIBs that may temporarily mask her pain.

Using LIBs interchangeably can sometimes make it much harder to notice that you have a problem. Instead of abusing one type of LIB to the point where it's obvious to others, switching between a variety of LIBs may not attract the same kind of attention. For example, one of my clients only drank on the weekend, so he never believed he was in denial about anything. But it was what he was doing during the rest of the week that bothered me. He was gambling every Monday night, hitting the strip clubs on Tuesday night, and indulging in petty theft at his workplace every Wednesday when his boss left early.

Individually these behaviors of his never appeared to be affecting his life in any way, but collectively they were weaving a tapestry of unrelated LIBs that was having just as negative an impact on his life—if not more so, in my opinion—than a single LIB would have done on its own.

REASON 2: INFREQUENCY

The second reason doing a seven-day denial audit doesn't work for every person is that some LIBs are simply not as detectable using a timeline or they never show up during the seven days. The reason? They may not take up excessive amounts of time, or they don't happen as often because they may need to be provoked by something in particular. These possibilities may explain the following LIBs:

- Most types of abuse, especially if the abuse is not recurring

- A debilitating phobia that shows itself only under specific circumstances, such as fear of traveling on the highway, fear of flying in planes, or fear of heights

- Certain types of psychological issues that arise only randomly or infrequently, such as seasonal affective disorder or panic attacks

- Anger or other emotions that need to be provoked

- Certain negative personal traits, such as racism, prejudice, greed, or trust issues

- Many health problems, especially those related to activities that don't necessarily happen during a typical week, such as diabetes, STDs, or allergies

REASON 3: SELF-DECEIT

As I stated in the beginning of this book, everyone is in denial about something that is causing their lives to be imbalanced. The third reason you may not have found your LIB could be that you're not letting yourself find it. You could be skewing the facts and dismissing certain actions, thoughts, and feelings to prevent yourself from seeing the truth.

If that's you—and I hope it's not—then none of the chapters thus far in part 2 will help you find your LIB because it's too easy for you to tamper with the results. That's why this final chapter in part 2 requires a little more attention from you. I promise you that following the rest of the advice in this chapter will keep you from sabotaging yourself.

LEARN TO TURN: THE FINAL FIVE STEPS THAT CAN FIND YOUR LIB

If you haven't found your LIB using all of my techniques up until now, then one of the three reasons I've just shown you—or a combination of the three—must be in play. That being the case, learning to turn to others around you whom you trust—as well as relying on a few experts—can finally grant you the answer you're looking for.

You don't have to take these steps, but bringing in not just one set of fresh eyes and ears but five sets of fresh eyes and ears, from five unique perspectives, is the ultimate way to flush out whatever LIB you're not addressing. If you're truly serious about changing your life and achieving the happiness we all crave and strive for, then this is your last chance. Please take what I'm about to ask of you seriously and do exactly what I'm about to ask of you.

1. Talk to Someone Who Loves You

Start by copying the list of LIBs from chapter 3—passive, aggressive, and severe. Then take that list to someone you know in your heart truly cares about you. The perfect choice is a family member or friend who has known you for a very long time and has absolutely nothing to gain by being dishonest with you.

Once you've chosen someone, show that person the list of LIBs and explain that you're looking to weed out any behaviors that may be unhealthy for you; then ask him or her if there is anything on the list that you may be suffering from and haven't recognized in yourself. Try not to be angry, hurt, or offended by what this person says. Remember, you asked for his or her help. Instead, extend your thanks afterward and be grateful that you may finally have an answer that will improve your life—and the life of your chosen person if this is someone you deeply care about.

2. Talk to Someone Who Likes You

Those who love us aren't always as honest as we'd like them to be, especially if they're afraid of hurting us with their honesty or of taking unnecessary blame for being the bearer of bad news. Going to a person who likes you but isn't so close that he or she feels timid telling you the truth can help you cover your bases.

Choose someone among your friends and acquaintances who's around you enough during the week to have an opinion about the way you act. Again, try to choose someone who has nothing to gain by lying to you. For example, a co-worker in the same position as you at your workplace may be a bad choice, since you never know if this person's LIB might be resentment toward you. Once you have your person, again, repeat the same steps as before: present the list, explain what you're trying to do, listen with an open mind, then thank the person for cooperating.

3. Talk to Someone Who Left You

This third person may be the hardest one for you to approach, since none of us ever feels entirely comfortable facing a person we no longer speak with. But if a friend or lover has ever walked out on you, claiming it was your fault, then take a huge leap of faith and believe that this person has some insight into you that your friends and family may not have or want to accept.

You won't need to present the list of LIBs to the person who left you since odds are that you won't be talking face-to-face. If possible, talking in person is ideal, but if either of you feel more relaxed having the conversation over the phone or through e-mail, that's fine as well. Once you're in contact with the person you picked, explain that you're in the process of improving yourself, emphasize that you don't want to make the same mistakes you've made in your past, and then ask if he or she was hurt by something about you that perhaps you could change.

Phrasing it in this way will open up the emotional doors a bit, since you will be showing that (1) you accept that you're not perfect and have made errors in your life, which your old friend or lover is well aware of, and (2) you value and respect this person's opinion. As with the first two people you ask for help, just listen, apologize for your past actions if you feel up to it, then thank the former friend or lover afterward.

4. Talk to a Physician

There's a reason many people hate going to the doctor, and it's not getting stuck with the scary sharp needles or sometimes having to waste your day waiting for them to see you. In most cases, it's because a good doctor may find something wrong with us that we don't want to know about. This step is obviously meant to ferret out only health-related issues or problems you may be ignoring or avoiding. Take it seriously and ask for a thorough head-to-toe examination, regardless of your age or current health.

5. Talk to a Psychologist

The last person to visit is someone most people fear. The stigma attached to visiting a therapist is a big deal to many people because they're scared of what others might think if they found out. Speaking with a trained psychologist, however, is an extremely healthy thing to do; it's also entirely confidential and a lot more common than you might think. If anything, simply look at a onetime visit to a therapist as an opportunity to get a 100 percent honest answer from a person who is sworn never to reveal anything you tell him or her and who you'll never have to see again. You'll be surprised at how cathartic it can be just to tell and be told the truth for a change!

When you go, bring your seven-day denial audit sheets for the professional to see, explain that you can't find anything wrong about your actions, and ask for an honest opinion. The therapist may notice patterns that you have failed to see or open your mind to other possibilities based on the areas of your life he or she has decided to explore.

Explain your intentions ahead of time, when you're making the appointment. Some therapists may require you to block out more than one session, or they may be fairly strict in how they handle their sessions. To find a good therapist in your area, look at the resources listed in chapter 18.

Part 3

Turning Denial into Balance

11

Finding and Facing Your Void

Your denial is a wall.

Your LIB is what's hiding behind that wall, secretly filling in for whatever has been missing in your life.

So what exactly is missing from your life? What's the emptiness within you that you need to fill with a LIB?

Once you finally know what your LIB is, you have to begin taking immediate steps to remove it from your life. That effort is the entire focus of the rest of this book, and it begins with this chapter. Breaking the denial in your life begins with finding—and facing—the void that you've been trying all this time to fill with a LIB.

WHAT'S LACKING IN YOUR LIFE?

There's an emptiness that's temporarily filled by whatever bad behaviors, actions, obsessions, or addictions you've been in denial about. That emptiness is the reason you obsessively fiddle with your Blackberry at a party instead of socializing. It's the reason you feel the need to tap things you bump into seven times before you can go about your day. It's why you turn to alcohol, food, drugs, anger, isolation, or ignorance in unhealthy ways that are affecting your life negatively. When you use a LIB, you feel a sense of relief because it distracts you from focusing on that emptiness. But a LIB's effects are only temporary, which is why we become so addicted to LIBs in the first place. We never get around to finding what's really missing in our lives so we can feel truly complete.

Something is missing inside you for reasons I can only guess at, since everyone's emptiness is unique. The emptiness may stem from your upbringing or from your current situation. It might be the result of a tragic event in your past. Regardless of what caused your emptiness, I can tell you that we all need to feel the same kinds of things inside ourselves in order to feel complete. If you have a LIB, you can be sure that you're missing at least one of the following things in your life.

A Clean Slate

What I mean by a "clean slate" is a life free of any major damage caused by any number of traumatic experiences.

- Is there something or someone in your past you will never forgive?

- Has something happened to you that you're afraid to speak to anyone about?

- Do you feel incomplete in some way—either physically or spiritually—because of something that happened in your past?

In our lives, all of us have experienced some type of physical, psychological, or emotional trauma, which naturally leaves its fair share of wounds behind. When dealt with properly and in a healthy manner, the wounds caused by trauma simply close up and heal over time, leaving us with a clean slate and a better perspective on life. But when those wounds go untreated, they begin to fester, open up, and create a void that only compounds the unhealed damage from the trauma.

That's when some deniers reach for a LIB to serve as a sort of bandage to help them heal. But a LIB never heals a wound. Instead, it only distracts you from the pain and prevents you from seeking the right treatment needed to close those wounds for good.

Comfort and Security

You've heard the expression "comfort food"? Well, being an emotional eater isn't the only LIB that is a source of instant support for some people. We all enjoy feeling protected—whether it's physically, financially, or spiritually. Knowing we have a steady job, sound relationships, and enough money and things to survive gives us a sense of safety and security that allows us to relax. But if one of those areas isn't stable—or any area that would normally bring you a feeling of security isn't reliable—it creates a void. That's when you might turn to a LIB to feel some sense of comfort. Let me ask you this:

- Do you always have a looming sense that an ax is about to fall?

- Do you feel a sense of abandonment or fear that you'll be abandoned one day?

- Are you always on edge about things that usually never happen?

There are many possible reasons for always having the mind-set that the other shoe is about to drop—even when the first shoe hasn't fallen yet. I've had clients who lived through hard times and have never felt completely secure since, even though they are doing fine financially. I've known people who were hurt so deeply by an ex-lover that it became impossible for them to completely trust anyone ever again. And I've seen people who watched a close friend suffer from a disease and ever since have feared that the same thing may happen to them.

Whatever the reason, not feeling that your world is stable can lead to a LIB. Some people turn to a LIB as a way to protect themselves from harm, such as being a workaholic, being stubborn or greedy, or being phobic about something. Other people choose LIBs that help them forget their uneasiness, such as washing away their worries by drinking or taking drugs. Either way, the LIB never addresses the real problem, which is why they feel vulnerable in the first place.

Control

All of us feel like our life is out of control from time to time. But when you spend every day feeling like there's a part of your life that's completely beyond your power to change, the frustration and help-lessness that may follow can be overwhelming. So ask yourself this:

- Do you feel powerless when it comes to making certain changes in your life?

- Is there something negative in your life right now (and not a LIB) that you feel helpless to remove?

- Is there someone in control of parts of your life who you feel shouldn't be?

Maybe you're in a relationship you can't walk away from, or it could be that you have a dead-end job that's making you feel trapped. Perhaps you have an oppressive parent or spouse who underestimates your abilities and won't let you make your own decisions or do anything on your own. What can happen in these types of situations—or in any situation that limits your ability to control your own destiny—is an urge to control something in order to feel like you're still free to choose. The problem? Just to feel in control, many people pick something to have power over—their appearance, their diet, their kids, their clean house—then obsess on it to the point that it's no longer healthy.

Happiness

So, are you happy? More important:

- Do you always carve out enough time to do what makes you happy?

- Did you land exactly where you hoped you would in life? If not, are you fine about that?

- Do you feel happy about something each and every day?

- Do you enjoy being around others as well as being alone?

- Does doing the things that made you happy ten years ago make you just as happy today?

The more of these questions you say no to, the greater are your chances of being unhappy about your life and depressed about it instead. That depression creates a void that needs to be filled, but instead of finding happiness from other things in life or from within yourself, like many people, you may have turned to a LIB. Granted, you may feel happy when using your LIB, but the moment you stop and the high disappears, you're left feeling even less happy than when you started.

A Purpose in Life

In order to move ahead in life, you need to point yourself toward a goal.

- Are you pursuing all—or at least some—of your dreams and ambitions?

- Do you feel your life is moving forward instead of just idling?

- Were you setting any plans in motion to improve your life prior to reading this book?

Everyone needs something off on the horizon to strive for, but when we either reach our goals or lack the drive to have them in the first place, we lose our sense of purpose. Having nothing to strive toward creates a huge void that leaves many people turning to LIBs out of depression or simply boredom.

Having something to look forward to is the key. My grandmother was a prime example of how anticipating something can keep you going. Her one desire was to see my sister get married. She had lived well beyond her years until that big day finally came. The next goal she had for herself was to travel cross-country to visit my sister. Once again, my grandmother found the will to stay alive longer than she was ever expected to and made the trip. After that, her next goal was to see my sister have her first baby. After the baby was born, however, my grandmother no longer had any new goals to look forward to. She ended up in the hospital, and I flew to see her and say my good-byes. She wasn't expected to make it through to the next day, but when she heard I was coming, she perked up for ten days afterward before she finally passed at the age of eighty-two. But what she left behind was a lesson: when you have a purpose in life, you always find the faith inside yourself to persevere and push on.

Resolution

Has anyone ever asked you a question, or told you a riddle, then left you high and dry to guess at the answer? Have you ever been told half of an interesting story, then interrupted before you could hear the rest of it? Only knowing half of something, without being able to instantly know the other half, can leave you feeling overly curious, anxious, and eventually frustrated.

Ask yourself these questions:

- Is there an issue or dilemma in my life that's never been addressed?

- Is there a question I've had for someone that's never been answered?

- Is there something I've been waiting to hear from someone but don't know when—or even if—I'll hear it?

Most of us feel a need to comprehend everything in our lives. When something prevents us from doing so, it can eat away at us and make us dwell on the half-finished puzzle forever. That "missing piece of the puzzle" becomes another void that we fill by reaching for a LIB.

I've watched grown adults whose parents separated when they were a child obsess for decades over why one parent didn't love them enough to stick around in their life. I've talked with people who've been rejected in love and had their hearts broken and who beat themselves up trying to understand why they weren't good enough to marry. But most commonly, I've spoken to many people who didn't achieve what they thought they would achieve in life and who spend their days second-guessing every action they ever made, trying to find where they took a misstep. Whatever your situation may be, for every answer you can't find in your life, odds are that you've replaced it with a LIB to help you forget what you don't have.

Self-Esteem

It feels good to be liked and accepted by those around you. But if you don't like and accept yourself, it creates a void in your life that no one can ever fill.

Ask yourself:

- Do I always place myself at fault for everything?

- Do I constantly feel useless and think I have nothing to offer others?

- Do I believe most people are better than I am in some way?

- Do I always feel that I never do enough, regardless of how hard I try?

- Do I believe that no matter what I do, no one ever notices my efforts?

- Do I always tell others what my flaws are?

Answering yes to any of these questions can easily indicate that you may think far less of yourself than you should. The fact of the matter is this: if you're not your biggest fan, it makes it virtually impossible to keep your life in balance. Low self-esteem keeps you from trying as hard to reach for the things that make you happy. It makes you believe you aren't worthy of having the positive things you deserve, and it prevents you from forging deep and honest relationships with others. After all, if you don't love yourself, it's very hard to believe that others can love you as well.

For some deniers, having low self-esteem can take an even darker turn and lead to self-loathing and self-hatred. A lot of deniers who suffer from severe LIBs—particularly addictions—seek out self-destructive behaviors. In fact, the more you hate yourself, the more likely you are to choose LIBs that are self-destructive as a way literally to punish yourself.

Have you ever wondered why some celebrities who seem to have everything in life—success, looks, money, fame—find themselves throwing it all away on aggressive LIBs such as drug or alcohol addiction? You'll see some celebrities blame Hollywood, or the temptations of being on the road, as the reason they find themselves in an unexpected state of self-destruction. But behind the scenes it may be that these celebrities and rock stars are really just trading in one LIB for another.

For some celebrities, it's the struggle to be successful that fills their void by giving them a sense of purpose or a feeling of self-worth. Once they reach the top and achieve success, however, they hit a ceiling. They can't go any further because they've achieved everything they set out to do. In fact, they can only go down from that point on. That's when some begin searching for other ways to fill the void that was originally filled by striving to achieve fame. They need to turn to something else to create that feeling of euphoria. Their LIBs may be different, but their underlying issue is usually the same.

NOW . . . THE GOOD NEWS!

Do you think you've figured out what may be missing in your life? Even if you're still not sure, that's okay. Before I tell you why, let me just share a story with you.

One of the best examples I can give you when it comes to filling a void is a good friend of mine. He grew up with parents who favored his siblings, so he never had much self-esteem. Instead, he grew up feeling neglected by his parents and always felt compelled to prove himself.

He may or may not have truly been neglected, but that didn't matter, because that's how he felt inside. So, to fill his void, he always needed to excel in everything he did. He enrolled in medical school, which was completely paid for by scholarships he had earned because of his exceptional grades. He became a very successful doctor and even acquired an ownership share in a hospital at an extraordinarily young age. With each new accomplishment, he was able to bolster his self-esteem temporarily and feel a sense of happiness. But the satisfaction he felt was always fleeting, leaving him no choice but to chase another bigger and better accomplishment to regain some sense of self-worth.

Once he reached the top of his profession, there was nothing left to do that would silence that feeling of worthlessness he had inside. Instead of enjoying his accomplishments, he could no longer quench that feeling—the same feeling that started as a child, continued throughout his life, and helped him achieve all of his successes. What was missing in his life was self-esteem, and when he ran out of accomplishments, he turned to using drugs to fill the void inside himself. Most people assumed that it was his high-stress job that led him down the road of drugs. In reality, it was his failure to address his void over all those years.

That's not going to happen to you. The rest of this book is designed to give you the tools you need to remove a LIB, but these tools go beyond that. They also can help you close whatever void exists inside you that's causing you to use a LIB in the first place. By implementing these tools,

- You'll finally take control of your life, and if you decide to go overboard using these tools, it will no longer be an unhealthy kind of excess. In fact, the more you use these tools, the better your life will become.

- You'll be shown how to rediscover your forgotten dream so that you can finally have a new purpose again.

- You'll learn how to find what makes you happy and how to draw more of it back into your life.

- You'll feel more secure than ever when you see how easy it is to reconnect with loved ones and ask them to help you beat your LIB.

- Your self-esteem will skyrocket because, by rebalancing yourself and removing your LIB, your life, and the lives of those around you, will drastically improve—all because of you.

- And finally, if my advice isn't enough to give you complete resolution with all of the unanswered questions in your life or a feeling that your slate is clean, I'll point you in the direction of reputable organizations and professionals who can heal the damage that may be beyond both of us.

12

Six Suggestions in Three Stages: Stage 1

Once you've shattered your wall of denial, discovered your LIB, and figured out what has been missing from your life, the next step is to fill that void inside you.

For decades addicts have been able to turn to twelve-step programs; based on a set of spiritual principles, these programs are designed to help addicts recover from the most severe LIBs, such as drug addiction, alcoholism, eating disorders, and other life-threatening behaviors. In fact, according to the American Medical Association, one of the most effective cures for addiction is a twelve-step program because it shows addicts how to stay out of denial by following a spiritual path in their lives. It's a formula that works, which is why it's used as a primary form of recovery for most addictive and compulsive behaviors worldwide. I've recommended twelve-step programs to those I've helped treat in the past, and I personally use the program to stay in control of my own LIBs.

Following some type of plan that mimics certain spiritual aspects of the twelve-step approach can be—and in my experience has proven to be—equally effective in putting an end to your LIB, regardless of what type of LIB you have. However, if you only suffer from a passive

LIB or an aggressive LIB that may not seem like a serious problem in your eyes, doing a twelve-step program can seem—and might be—a bit over the top.

If that's you, then ask yourself this question: How serious am I about getting my life to a place where I'm far happier than I've ever been? I suggest that you ask yourself this question because even the most passive LIB can throw your life out of balance and keep you from getting or achieving certain things that you deserve. Even the most passive LIB can affect the areas of your life that matter most, such as your health, your finances, and your relationships. Yes, even the most passive LIB can change your life in negative ways that you're not even aware of.

The point is that taking the right spiritual approach is one proven way, experts feel, to treat the most extreme LIBs. Maybe you feel that your LIB doesn't deserve that type of attention, but I do, and I guarantee that those closest to you feel the same way. By modifying some of the most powerful steps used by experts in the addiction field and combining them with a few tried-and-true suggestions that have helped those I've taught over the years, it is possible to treat—and beat—any LIB you may have, no matter how passive or severe it is.

BEFORE YOU START

Once you've broken through your wall of denial, your first instinct may be to rejoice, but that's where most deniers make the biggest mistake. You have only a small window of time before the bricks you've torn down begin slowly—or rapidly for some deniers—to fall right back into place.

Once you finish reading this book and place it on the shelf, a clock will begin to tick away. Every minute you waste not taking charge of your life shifts your life further out of balance. It's easy to let distractions pull you back into denial—after all, that's what denial does. It helps you find excuses for why you're not taking the right actions in your life. That's why, if you don't have an immediate plan of action, everything you've learned about yourself from this point forward isn't going to be of use to you.

The six suggestions I'm about to give you in the next few chapters should be implemented as quickly as possible. In a perfect world, you would get all six started in one day. However, depending on your LIB, some of them may take more time. That's why I'm going to ask you to do all six in three stages. Stage 1 is one suggestion that you need to start today: as soon as you're through reading this chapter, put down this book and immediately begin doing exactly what it asks you to do. Once you're finished, you can proceed to stages 2 and 3 (described in the following two chapters). Stage 2 will have two suggestions for what you need to do, while stage 3 will have the last three suggestions.

Now let's begin!

SUGGESTION 1: OWN YOUR DENIAL ON PAPER

Whether you believe it or not, remember this: you are in control of your own denial. You are in control of your LIB. The only real question is this: now that you know what you've been bringing to the table all these years, are you strong enough to admit that what's been holding you back is you yourself? Right now is when you absolutely need to answer yes.

When it comes to your LIB, there is no such thing as maybe—the answer is either yes or no. If you can't own up to who you are, what your LIB is, and the fact that you are the one calling its shots, you are staying in denial. You are continuing to let denial control your life instead of being in charge of your life yourself. As long as you stay in denial, your odds of ever recovering, no matter how passive, aggressive, or severe your LIB is, drop to zero.

That's why you need to own your denial by writing it down in a letter to yourself, one that includes every detail about how your denial has affected you and those around you in a negative way. You may be wondering, Why should I write it down? Can't I just lay all the cards on the table? After all, I know what my LIB is now, so why go to the effort of placing something on paper that someone else might see?

Actually, that's exactly why I want you to do it. And the person who needs to find that piece of paper—each and every day—is you.

Once most people overcome a LIB, their first reaction is to want to forget about how their behaviors hurt themselves and those around them. I've known addicts who, after finally admitting their addictions, expected their friends and family to never bring it up again because it might trigger them to start again. But they were all wrong. You may think that remembering your LIB will make you regretful or angry toward yourself. But it's remembering how out of balance your LIB made your life that is a critical step in preventing it from shifting your life out of balance ever again.

If you don't own your denial by writing it on paper, it has a way of creeping back into your life, clouding your memory of how out of balance your life really was. It becomes easier to forget some—if not all—of the negative behaviors and bad incidents you meant to watch out for, and you become more susceptible to them if they resurface again. It becomes easier to forget about the people who were hurt by your LIB, making you more likely to hurt them again—and possibly lose them forever. It becomes easier to forget that you were ever to blame—in fact, over time you may remember all the circumstances yet completely rewrite who was actually at fault.

Having your denial spelled out in detail on a sheet of paper gives you something to turn to. It serves as an instant reminder of how your LIB has affected your life so that you never forget. It makes it impossible to ignore your denial when every action, every emotion, and every negative effect caused by your LIB is laid out right there in front of you. But most important, writing down your denial can begin to close any type of void, especially a void caused by not feeling in control and having no purpose in life. Owning your denial gives you more control over your life—as well as a game plan for achieving a new, healthy direction in life.

Getting Started

Step 1. Write down your LIB, your void, and your intentions

The first step is simple: at the top of the sheet of paper, all I want you to do is write down three short sentences to yourself:

- Write down what your LIB is.

- Write down what your void is.

- Finally, tell yourself that you want to be back in balance.

For example, using some of the most common LIBs from the ADAPT list in chapter 2, you might write down something that looks like the following:

Abuse
I'm being abused.
My void is self-esteem.
I want to be back in balance.

Disorders
I've got a debilitating phobia about flying.
My void is security.
I want to be back in balance.

Addiction

I'm an alcoholic.

My void is having a purpose in life.

I want to be back in balance.

Physical issues

I'm ignoring that I may have diabetes.

My void is control.

I want to be back in balance.

(The) Truth

I have severe trust issues.

My void is having a clean slate.

I want to be back in balance.

Step 2. Make a list of the damage that's been done

Going as far back as you can remember, write down all of the negative things that have happened as a direct result of your denial and your LIB. To make it easier, try to break these negative effects down by category, such as how your LIB has affected your family, your work, your health, your relationships, your reputation, your personal time, and finally, how you feel about yourself.

For each category, try to think about all the different ways in which your LIB may have affected you, such as

- Were there any important events, appointments, or moments that you missed?

- Were there any people you hurt or people who no longer speak to you?

- Were there any opportunities you lost out on that could have made your life better?

Step 3. Make a list of all your triggers

There are certain events, people, or key situations that can leave you more susceptible to using your LIB. For example, if you're an alcoholic, there are probably a number of things that trigger your urge to drink—such as hanging with a best friend who drinks, going out with your co-workers for business lunches, or watching the big game on TV every Sunday.

You need to be aware of all of your triggers so that you'll know which individuals, places, or circumstances tempt you to use your LIB. To start, grab your seven-day denial audit, find all of the moments when you used your LIB, and then look at what was happening right before it.

- Did something specific happen to you immediately before you used your LIB? For instance, did you bump into someone or meet up with anyone?

- Did something upset you emotionally?

- Were you thinking about something that made you anxious, mad, or sad?

- Was it a situation where not engaging in your LIB would have made you feel awkward?

Once you've identified a possible trigger, write it down, then leave a few empty lines underneath it. (You'll need this space later.) Keep listing all of your triggers from your seven-day denial audit; when you're finished, try to expand your list by writing down other things you can think of that may not have happened during your denial audit. One way to get the ball rolling is by answering this question about yourself: "I once got the urge to use my LIB when. . . ."

For example, if your LIB is financial irresponsibility and getting yourself deeper in debt, answering that question might help jog your memory of a certain store with high-ticket items that make you itch to spend money when you visit it. Or maybe it was browsing eBay while at work, reading a magazine that flaunts a lot of cool products you wish you owned, or hanging with a certain friend who spends money just as frivolously as you do.

After you've identified as many triggers as possible, start at the top of the list and for each trigger think of a few options healthier than your LIB that you can turn to the next time you're faced with it. For example, if you always have a smoke after you eat, write down a healthier activity you can do that relaxes you just as much as a few cigarettes, like calling a friend who always makes you laugh. If your drinking buddy invites you out, write down that you'll only meet him in a place where alcohol isn't served. If hearing sad songs leaves you depressed, make a note to remove them from your iPod. Keep running through your list of triggers until you've written a few alternatives to your LIB underneath each one.

Step 4. Keep the list close and read it often

Depending on how severe your LIB is, owning your denial may take only a page or two, or you may be left with a ream of sheets when all is said and done. Regardless of the size of your list, the information you've written there is something you need to have with you at all times. It's the first thing I want you to read in the morning, so that you're always reminded of who you are and the LIBs you're trying to eliminate from your life.

It's also a tool to turn to whenever you're challenged with a tempting situation that may evoke your LIB. Having the list on hand can remind you of other options to rely on when you can't always rely on yourself. If it's too unwieldy to carry on you, then try making a miniaturized copy that lists only your triggers, the alternative reactions for each trigger, and a few of the worst things that happened as a result of your LIB. Just make sure that you have some version of the list on you at all times.

PUT IT IN YOUR OWN HANDWRITING

No matter how computer-literate you may be, no matter how poor you think your penmanship is, it's important that you write this letter by hand. Why? The answer's easy: what's more thoughtful to you—a thank-you note sent by e-mail or one that comes to you written out in a letter or card?

Admitting your denial and revealing how it has affected your life on paper is a thousand times more meaningful. Especially when you remember that this piece of paper is meant to be a reminder to yourself—from yourself—to never again return to that place of denial in your life. So grab a pen and keep it personal. That way, it will be that much more powerful each and every time you read it.

Step 5. Remember that the list is a work in progress

Just because you've written down on your list every trigger that initially came to mind doesn't mean you can't add anything else you may think of later on. In fact, when you read the list each morning, I want you to consider whether anything has happened recently that made you anxious to turn to your LIB. Or perhaps there's something else you didn't think of when you first wrote everything down. If so, then add those triggers to the list, even if that requires writing it out all over again.

You may not remember some of the worst damage your LIB has caused because you may not be completely aware yet of how your LIB has affected everyone around you. You may not know all your triggers because there may be some you've forgotten or new ones about to head your way. As new ones come to you, just be sure to add them to your list.

13

Stage 2: Set Up
Your Circle of Trust

You're not in this alone.

Even though I asked you in stage 1 to own your denial on paper, that doesn't mean you'll be trying to eliminate your LIB all by yourself. The fact of the matter is that you can't do it all by yourself, which is why you need to start recruiting the right people to help you out. That's what stage 2 is all about.

As soon as you read this chapter, the same rules apply that applied to stage 1. Immediately stop reading the book so that you can implement these two suggestions. However, because these suggestions may take more time (depending on your LIB), you have up to two weeks to accomplish them. After they're completed, you can move on to stage 3.

SUGGESTION 2: SET UP YOUR CIRCLE OF TRUST

Once you've broken down the wall of denial and know your LIB, it's crucial that you ask for support from others to help keep you from rebuilding your wall. You need to select the right people to help you stay on track—people who are not only the ones in whom you confide but the ones you can turn to without fail, since you never know when a moment of weakness will hit you. That's why I call this group of individuals your "circle of trust."

Getting Started

Picking the right people to join your circle of trust can make or break your effort to put an end to your LIB.

How many people you choose to have in your circle is up to you, although between five and six is a good place to start. Some people can feel awkward, as if they're always under the microscope, if they create a circle of trust that's too big (eight people or higher). Having too many people in your circle of trust can also set you up for hearing too many differing opinions on how to handle your LIB. It's entirely fine to stick with fewer people, so long as you feel that the core of your group is solid.

If you don't have enough people in your life to create a circle of trust made up of five to six individuals, that's fine as well. A circle of trust doesn't have to be that big if you don't have many individuals to pick from. If you don't believe me, then remember that many hard-core addicts typically have just one sponsor in their corner. The numbers don't really matter, but finding people with the right attributes is key, especially because you're about to share your denial with each person you place in your circle of trust.

Here are my must-know ground rules on how—and who—to choose.

DO pick people who aren't afraid of you

You'll be giving those in your circle of trust full clearance to call you on any actions they believe may lead you to slip back into your LIB.

That's why you need to choose people who aren't scared to do so. The stronger the people you choose, the stronger the support they'll be able to offer you when you need it most. People who have noticed your LIB in the past and had no problem mentioning it to you are ideal for your circle of trust—so long as neither of you harbors any resentment from the past.

DON'T pick anyone who stands to benefit—or lose—from being in your circle of trust

The people you pull into your circle of trust should only be those who can't benefit from letting you stay in denial or lose by helping you break free of it. For example, if your LIB is work addiction, asking your business partner to be in your circle of trust wouldn't be wise, no matter how close you are with that person, because helping you beat your LIB could hurt the business. If your LIB is mishandling your money, it may not be wise to ask certain family members or friends who have been enjoying all your expensive gifts to them to help you change your spending habits. I once knew a person who thought it was perfectly fine to ask his drinking buddies (who weren't alcoholics) for support with getting his sobriety under control. He couldn't understand that, even though they could control their own drinking, helping him could lead to the loss of a friend they enjoyed hanging out with, and that possibility could make them more likely to let him slide every once in a while.

Each person you choose should be someone who can't benefit or lose in any way by allowing your LIB to continue; otherwise, you will never trust them to be sincere. If possible, ask those who will benefit by putting an end to your LIB to join your circle. You'll know that the opinions of these people are genuine, because helping you means helping themselves as well.

DO make sure you have 24/7 support

All it takes is one moment of weakness to spiral back into denial. Some of your friends may not be available at certain critical times when you need them the most because of factors such as their work or family schedule, an upcoming vacation, or a time zone difference. That's why it's especially wise to choose people with a variety of schedules, so that the greatest amount of flexibility is built into your circle of trust. Break down your typical week hour by hour, and ask yourself who you could turn to during each hour. Using your seven-day denial audit can help—just look at each activity and ask yourself who you could have relied on for support at that moment.

There are other good ways to ensure around-the-clock support. Having some friends on the opposite coast in your circle of trust can be extremely helpful. Being a few hours behind or ahead of the members of your circle is convenient, especially if the urge to fall back into your LIB hits while most of your local friends are asleep or at their nine-to-five job. Also, having one person in your circle of trust who's a co-worker can be advantageous—as long as your need for support doesn't compromise your co-worker's work or jeopardize his or her job (or yours) in any way.

I suggest to my clients that ideally they should have at least three to four people they can count on at any hour of the day or night in their circle of trust. Having this many people sets up an instant backup system if your number one choice isn't always available. It will also give you more freedom to rotate through those in your circle of trust so that you're not always calling on the same few people every time. That can cause a problem, which is why I always recommend the next tip.

DON'T rely on the same person 24/7

The problem with placing too much responsibility on a single individual in your circle of trust is that many deniers begin to feel guilty over time for burdening one person. That can make them less likely to turn to their friend for help and support when they need that person the most.

DO pick someone who shares your LIB—and is in control of it

As you choose people to be in your circle of trust, you'll also be revealing your LIB to them. It's at that time that you should ask each person if they share the same LIB that you're dealing with. Some people may freely reveal that personal information to you before you even ask, while others may say no because they're in denial about their LIB and don't know it yet. But if you can find someone who has already gone through the process of beating their LIB and made it through to the other side, consider yourself blessed.

Having at least one person in your circle of trust who has been through the same experience—or at least something similar—not only gives you access to whatever he or she knows about coping with your LIB, but serves as proof that there is hope of overcoming it. On the other hand, avoid choosing a person for your circle of trust who you suspect has your LIB but still isn't strong enough to admit it.

DON'T pick anyone who shares your LIB but is still in denial

Granted, everyone you choose for your circle of trust has their own LIB, since all of us do, but choosing someone who suffers from the same LIB that you do, but who doesn't admit that they have a LIB, can hold you back on many levels.

First, it's hard to be advised by someone who's equally guilty of making the same mistakes you've made but opts to do nothing about them. You need to be able to look up to and respect those in your circle of trust, and taking advice from someone who's incapable of doing what you're trying to do isn't a smart way to start overcoming your LIB.

Second, that person could end up sabotaging your efforts on purpose. Have you ever heard the expression, "Misery loves company"? Well, denial makes misery look like a loner. Those in denial of a LIB aren't always thrilled to see others trying to beat the same LIB because those efforts indirectly point a finger at their own behaviors. The more people they see using their LIB, the more their own actions seem entirely normal. That's why you should only pick people who either have had your LIB and beaten it or people who don't share your LIB and who know that it's unhealthy for you.

DO pick a few people who can see you

It's fine if some of the people you plan to use in your circle of trust aren't local—such as certain family members or close friends who live in another city, state, or country—as long as someone you pick is nearby.

It's important to choose a few people who have access to you and your life and who see you regularly enough to know if you seem distant, angry, depressed, or upset. If possible, choose a few people who see you in different settings during the day, since you may be more susceptible to a LIB at different times during the day. For example, choose your roommate, but also choose a co-worker or someone involved in the same social groups or activities you're involved in. Anyone you trust will do.

DON'T pick anyone who doesn't come free

If you're asked (or you just feel compelled) to give someone in your circle of trust something in return for their help—such as doing them a favor or lending them a little money—don't include them. Even though you may feel it's the right thing to do for someone who's being supportive of you, it places that person in a position of gaining something from you the longer you remain in denial. This rule doesn't apply when it comes to hiring a professional counselor, therapist, or other type of adviser to help you with your LIB.

HOW TO ASK THE RIGHT WAY

Approaching others for help may seem like a daunting, awkward, and embarrassing task, but let's be honest: since many of the people you'll choose are most likely people you're very close to, you can assume that most of them are already fully aware of your LIB. Most of the people you ask will probably be extremely grateful that you're finally doing something about your LIB and will consider it an honor to be part of an effort to help you beat it—as long as you approach them in the right way.

- *Give them the truth:* Begin by explaining that you're aware of your LIB and looking to place your behaviors behind you once and for all. Next, tell them what they mean to you and why you chose them, so that they're aware of just how much you trust them. Then ask if they might be willing to help you with the process.

- *Give them permission:* Let them know that you're allowing them complete freedom to call you out for your actions at any time if they see you falling back into your LIB.

- *Give them a promise:* Some people may not believe you won't hold a grudge if they say or do the wrong thing toward you. That could cause them to not be as honest with you when it comes to offering advice or telling you when they feel you're slipping up. So tell them that you value their opinions—or else you would have never asked them—and then make them a solid promise that you won't hold any grudges and will listen with an open mind and heart.

- *Give them a choice:* You may find that a few people won't be interested in being a part of your circle of trust. Before you ask them for a yes or no answer, let them know that you won't be disappointed if they choose not to get involved.

- *Give them your thanks:* Whether they say yes or no, thank anyone you ask to be a member of your circle of trust for considering it. Not only is it the right thing to do, but you may find that someone who initially said no turns around and says yes later on. Remember, you may be approaching someone who's battling the same LIB and for their own reasons may not be comfortable with what you're asking. Or you could be asking someone who's still upset with you for things that happened because of your LIB. By ending the conversation with a thank-you, you increase your chances of gaining their support eventually, which can only strengthen your circle of trust.

SUGGESTION 3: CREATE A DENIAL CONTRACT

If you're serious about removing your LIB, you need to set up a denial contract with someone that gives that person permission to take action on your behalf should you start rebuilding your wall of denial. For example, I have a contract with my family, which can be acted on by two or more relatives on my list; it states that if I ever again take any mind-altering substances, they legally have the right to take over and handle all matters having to do with my mental well-being. That means signing me into a drug treatment center—where I have to give up my rights—as well as taking over my finances and my company. I've actually signed over power of attorney to my parents—that's how much I believe in a denial contract. I've now been clean and sober since 1989—that's how well it works!

The consequences of my own denial contract may seem extreme, but then again, my LIBs were severe and life-threatening. Your LIB may be a passive or an aggressive one that doesn't require such harsh measures. But no matter what your LIB is, establishing a contract that has a cause-and-effect provision is a valuable deterrent should you slide back into using your LIB at any time.

The Co-Signer: Who Should You Choose?

By creating your circle of trust, you've already rounded up people who (1) have nothing to gain by watching you fail, (2) will be available to offer any advice or support you need, and (3) aren't afraid to tell you when you've tripped up. Now you need to find the right person from your circle who will hold you accountable for your actions if you fail to stick to your word and fall back into your LIB.

That person should be someone who you feel won't be judgmental but who will stick to their guns when it comes to handling the arrangements you agree to in your contract. A spouse isn't always the best choice; a parent, sibling, sponsor, or close friend is a better pick. One technique I use with clients who can't decide who to ask is this: imagine who you would want to be in charge of your well-being if you were ever in a car accident and incapable of making decisions for yourself. Within your circle of trust, who's the person you would want to be the one deciding whether to flip the switch on your life support or not? Whoever comes immediately to mind is the person to ask to be your co-signer.

The Provisions of Your Contract

Your contract could be as simple as a one-page, handwritten agreement, or it could be as complex as a multi-page legal document drawn up by an attorney (which is my recommendation for anyone dealing with a serious, life-threatening, LIB). Anything that involves money or a reversal of rights should be handled by an attorney, regardless of the LIB.

It's important to make the details in your contract as specific as possible to start. Down the road, when you have a track record of sticking to it, you can opt to rewrite the contract with your co-signer. But, for now, the contract you type out needs to contain all of the following provisions.

Provision 1. Make a plan to get help for your LIB immediately

This book and the advice it offers count as help, but you may need to add some extra assistance to the bargaining table, such as promising to visit an outpatient center, a financial adviser, a psychologist, or a physician, depending on what your LIB is. Taking this step is wise not just to help speed up your recovery from your LIB but to show your co-signer that you are serious about what you're about to do.

Provision 2. Compile a list of rules that should never be broken

The most obvious rule is to not succumb to your LIB, but there are plenty of other rules that should be clearly spelled out, especially when it comes to staying clear of anything that may trigger your LIB. That's where the letter you wrote to yourself in the last chapter comes in handy—as a reminder that you own your denial.

Many of the triggers you've already written down in that letter can easily be turned into rules spelled out in your contract that are never to be broken. For example, if one of your triggers is hanging with a certain friend or contacting certain people, then one of your rules could be to stop speaking to these friends, or to speak to them only in the presence of someone in your circle of trust. Take the time to review all of your triggers and then ask your co-signer if he or she can think of any others that might help keep you on track.

Provision 3. Set a consequence for breaking each rule

It should be clearly spelled out what will happen if you break any of the rules in your contract. The severity of your LIB should equal the severity of the consequences as spelled out in the contract. For me, my old LIBs would kill me if I ever went back to them. That's why, in the contract with my parents, I lose everything if I go back on my word. The more serious your LIB is, the more serious the rules, restrictions, and consequences should be—and the more rigorously they should be enforced, even if that means "by law." If you have a passive or aggressive LIB that isn't as serious, then the rules, restrictions, and consequences can be less harsh, but your LIBs should be given just as much consideration as severe ones. For example,

- Some of my clients have agreed to lose something to charity, such as something they owned or a certain amount of money, which was then placed in the hands of the co-signer.

- I've known people in denial about their health problems who offered to give others permission to access their medical records so they could check how often the denier was going for medical help and find out what was going on with the denier's health.

- The consequences may be a more intensive version of the help you agreed to get at the start of the contract. For example, if you agreed to seek help on an outpatient basis, the consequences for breaking the rules may be to immediately check in to an inpatient program.

- The consequences may even be as extreme as giving your co-signer the right to call the authorities on you if you continue a LIB that's illegal.

Provision 4. Create a check-in schedule

In the contract, you need to establish a schedule for checking in with your co-signer to let that person know how you're doing. You may agree to call or meet up in person every day or every week, depending on your situation. Perhaps you agree to call at certain times when you're more susceptible to your LIB. Regardless of its details, the schedule should be one that both of you agree to and can stick to.

Provision 5. Sign the contract (both of you)

I've known some deniers with severe LIBs who had attorneys draft an official agreement so that they would be legally accountable for their actions. You probably don't require that much red tape, but regardless, signing your name to your contract, then having your co-signer do the same, makes it official and adds a seriousness to the contract between the two of you that can help you stick to its rules.

THE MORE, THE MERRIER

If you wish, you can have multiple co-signers on your contract. In fact, having more than one co-signer can give you added security in case one co-signer turns out to be not strong enough to enforce the rules. Having a few people with power over certain aspects of your life may also make you accept the repercussions a little more easily than would be the case if that power was placed in the hands of just one individual. Instead of being tried in front of a judge, you're undergoing something more like a trial by jury. After all, if several people say you've broken the contract, it becomes harder to deny it.

Once the contract has been written and signed, make copies for both you and your co-signer. Then you need to place your contract right along with your letter in a place where you can see it and read it each and every day. Don't tuck it away in a safe place because, like the letter, it's meant to serve as a daily reminder of what you're trying to do.

14

Stage 3: Bringing Back the Balance

Thanks to stage 1, you've already owned your denial, made a list of the damage it caused, and determined what triggers your LIB. Thanks to stage 2, you now have a group of people you can trust to support you when you need it—and to hold you accountable if you blow it. Now, in stage 3, it's time to make a few necessary changes to your life that will quickly restore some balance to it.

The three suggestions in this chapter can help you plant the seeds that will eventually grow into a more positive direction for your life. All it takes is reprioritizing your time, reconnecting with the right people, and reclaiming the dream you somehow left behind. You already have the will. You already have the support. Now you will have the tools to bring back the balance that can keep your LIB in check.

As with the last two chapters, you should begin implementing the changes discussed here immediately after reading the chapter. Try to make these changes in two weeks time, if possible.

SUGGESTION 4: FIND WHAT MAKES YOU HAPPY

Everyone has a purpose in life, so what's yours?

For me, my purpose turned out to be helping others just like myself. But when I got clean and sober, I thought the way to be happy was through relationships and success. I thought that sur-rounding myself with as many people as possible would make me feel connected. I spent hours in the gym working out, trying to look my best in order to attract others. I worked several jobs at once, slogging through twelve-hour days back-to-back for weeks on end, chasing the almighty dollar. I thought that having plenty of money and friends would finally eliminate the insecurities I felt within me by somehow validating my self-worth. But you know what? None of it ever did.

I eventually realized that it was taking people from the darkness of their addictions and bringing them into the light of understanding that truly made me happy. So I gave up a well-paying job in market-ing for a minimum-wage job at a nonprofit organization that handled addictions to drugs and alcohol. It was a struggle at the start, but for the first time in my life I was happy. My life finally came into bal-ance, and once it did, everything I'd been desperately seeking—the relationships, the success—not only fell into place on their own but suddenly didn't seem all that necessary to my happiness anymore.

So again, I ask you, what's your purpose in life? Or more simply, what makes you happy? Somewhere along the way you must have lost it, because chasing your dreams takes time and effort that anyone with a LIB simply doesn't have. Recapturing your purpose in life and finding what used to make you happiest can fill all your voids at once.

If you're like some people, figuring out what makes you happy isn't the easiest thing to do. As time went by, maybe you forgot your dream, or gave up chasing it. Maybe you were one of the lucky ones who managed to achieve your dream, yet suddenly found yourself unsatisfied. Somehow your dream never lived up to your expectations; then you were left with no dream at all to chase.

Being without a dream—or not bothering to go after one—is fuel to a LIB. It creates every type of void and leaves us reaching for behaviors that can help us forget what we feel we'll never achieve, deserve, or have. That's why it's critical to figure out—then reestablish—your forgotten dream right away.

Imagine That Money Is Not an Obstacle

I ask my clients to imagine that they have access to all of the money in the world. I ask them to picture waking up every day and having the financial means to accomplish anything they want to do.

What would you do under these conditions? How would you fill up your day if you didn't have to worry about making a living?

So what did you come up with? Everyone knows instinctively what makes them happy, and most of us can also think of other things we believe might make us happy but we have yet to try them. For most of us, a list of things that make us happy may seem impossible to do because of time or finances, but many of the things that truly make us happy are easily attainable.

People dismiss many of their dreams and passions because they think they lack the time to pursue them, but the time is always there, especially if you're a victim of a LIB. And when it comes to having enough money, some of my clients have in fact had the type of financial freedom I've asked you to imagine, yet their LIB still prevented them from realizing their dreams.

You may not be able to remember all of your forgotten dreams immediately. But by taking the time you usually invest in your LIB and spending it instead on one or two of your dreams, you'll be placing yourself back on the path toward a goal that will ultimately make you happy. You may not be able to achieve the dream at the level you wish for—like having the freedom to travel the world for the rest of your life—but the pursuit of your dream can be just as satisfying as achieving it.

Go Back in Time

Sometimes it's difficult to pinpoint exactly what would make you happier than you are now. That's why one of the quickest ways to find your forgotten dreams is to step back and examine your life from the beginning to the present.

Grab every photo you have of yourself from the time you were born until the present, place them in chronological order, and then start with the first picture of yourself at an age when you remember having any type of dreams or aspirations. As you look at each picture, I want you to ask yourself four things:

- Was I happy then?

- If so, what made me happy at that time?

- If not, what was happening in my life that made me unhappy?

- Either way, was my life in true balance?

What I mean by "true balance" in the last question is this: Was your life really all about work or school? Or was your life divided up in such a way that you were spending equal time getting everything you needed emotionally?

As you continue to go through your life in pictures, write down the days, months, and years when you were happier than you are now. Then look at what you were doing and who was in your life then. With the exception of those who've passed away, you would be surprised at how many activities, people, places, and things from your past can be brought back into your life if you simply take the time to do so.

Don't Look at the Actions—Look at the Emotions

Sometimes it's impossible to return to the things that made you the happiest you've ever been. Your happiest years may have been when certain people were still alive, when you were at the top of your class, or when you still had high hopes of becoming a successful movie actress, a big baseball star, or some other out-of-reach dream that reality brought to an end. These are dreams you can never get back. But what you can do is look at why they made you feel happy in the first place.

When you take a close look at what you've lost that once filled your life with joy, you'll find that, underneath, your joy was based on one of three possible feelings: security from feeling loved and needed; self-worth from feeling a sense of pride and accomplishment; or satisfaction from knowing you were moving forward and had a purpose. As you look at what brought you happiness in the past, decide which of these three feelings was attached to that activity, person, or place. Then try to think of new activities, people, or places that would evoke those same emotions today.

For example,

- Was it the specific people in your life who made you happy or the fact that you felt loved, protected, and needed? You may never have those loved ones back, but you can recapture that sense of belonging and love through new, healthy, relationships.

- Was it being the best and brightest in your class, or was it the boost to your self-esteem that you got from your academic accomplishments? Maybe you're no longer the smartest person

in town, but there are plenty of other things you may be able
to succeed at that could make you feel talented once more.

- Was it thinking you would be an actress or baseball star that
  made you happy, or was it believing you might actually achieve
  what you set out to do? You may never be famous, but you can
  recapture that feeling by making plans to achieve other, more
  realistic, goals you've always had that might be easier to attain.

Examining the emotions you felt when you were happy in the past
can give you a better blueprint of the feelings—not activities—that
you need to start adding to your life. I'll admit that you're certainly
not in the same situation you once enjoyed. In many ways, I wouldn't
recommend trying to re-create your past, because that can mean
taking several steps back from where you've come. Trying to re-create
the past is often part of the problem for people who never seem to
move on with their lives. They get stuck in a time warp, doing the
things they used to do years ago because they are trying to re-create
that feeling of happiness they once had. The mistake they make is
in repeating the activities they once enjoyed instead of trying to feel
security, self-worth, and satisfaction through new activities.

As I mentioned earlier, three of the happiest years of my life were
spent managing a nonprofit organization that dealt with drug and
alcohol addiction. Many years later, when I found myself looking for
a new purpose in life, a friend pointed out that the happiest he'd ever
seen me was when I was working there. None of the other jobs I'd
held compared to that time when I was helping others get into recovery. I couldn't go back to that job because it would have been several
steps backward in my career, but I was able to achieve the same emotions I felt back then by becoming the interventionist I am today. It's
not the same job by any means, but it's equally fulfilling because I
once again feel needed, I feel proud of my work, and I feel like I'm
moving forward in my life.

SUGGESTION 5: APOLOGIZE TO THOSE WHO HAVE BEEN HURT BY YOUR DENIAL

You're not the only one who's been hurt by your denial: those around you, especially the ones who care (or cared) about you, have been hurt as well. Once you've broken yourself free of denial, it's vital to make a conscious effort to make amends to anyone who may have been affected by your LIB. Writing a list of everyone you can think of who may have been hurt by your LIB—family members, co-workers, friends, even brief acquaintances from your past—and then taking the effort to say you're sorry is an incredibly crucial action for two reasons.

First, *apologizing turns your bricks into glass*. By admitting to another person that you've been in denial, you make it impossible to fall into denial as easily ever again. It's much harder to use denial as a shield between you and someone else once you've confessed the truth about your LIB. By apologizing to those who have been hurt by your LIB, you instantly shatter any wall of denial you ever had between yourself and those individuals.

If you try to slide back into your old habits and begin grabbing bricks to rebuild your wall, you'll discover that having admitted your LIB and apologized for it has transformed your bricks of denial into glass. Any wall you try to rebuild will hide nothing, because it's now transparent. Everyone can see through your glass wall of denial, which makes it much more fragile and easier to tear down in the future.

Second, *apologizing turns every person into a nail*. The more out of balance your life is, the more likely it is that it will eventually fall apart, if certain parts of it haven't already. However, finally owning your denial on paper is the support beam that's now bracing your life. It's the underpinning of a fresh start—a more balanced life and a healthier you. That's why I like to have my clients imagine that the act of admitting their LIB and apologizing to those they've hurt turns each of those individuals into a nail—a nail driven directly into that support beam to hold it in place and keep it from buckling.

The more people you can be honest with and apologize to, the more nails you'll drive into that support beam to keep it from budging. And the more nails you have in that beam, the more likely you are to feel

- Less regret, because each nail brings resolution

- Less unhappy, because you're reuniting with those you may have lost along the way

- Less empty, because each of these people helps to fill a little piece of your void

Getting Started

Once you have your list of people to approach, the actual process may feel intimidating. But you must realize that if you've hurt someone with your LIB, that person is 100 percent aware of your LIB and has discussed it with others, whether you're aware of it or not. What should bring you comfort is knowing that revealing and apologizing for your LIB makes it possible for those you care about to feel as if they can discuss your LIB with you directly and not behind your back. It puts an end to the gossip and starts the process of healing. Instead of beating you down with how your behaviors have hurt them, they are now able to lift you up and carry you through your recovery process.

Step 1. Admit your LIB, and then apologize for it

Yes, each person on your list already knows what you're about to say, but remember that you hurt this person in the past because you were never in agreement about your LIB and the damage it was causing. Admitting your LIB before you apologize lets the person know that the two of you are finally on the same page.

Step 2. Ask for a list of grievances

The best way to turn someone affected by your LIB into a nail that can help you overcome it is through a fresh start. For that to happen, the slate you have with that person has to be wiped clean.

Just because you think you know how your LIB affected someone else doesn't necessarily mean that you're completely aware of how destructive it was to that person. If you never fully grasp how many problems your LIB caused in that individual's life, your apology may seem less sincere, even though your intentions are pure. Not addressing every issue simply because you don't want to hear about every way in which your LIB hurt someone else may also prevent that person from being supportive of you later on.

That's why, right after your apology, you need to ask that person to thoroughly explain how your LIB was hurtful or upsetting. Tell the person that you want to apologize again for everything, not just the damage you remember, so that you can offer the level of apology he or she rightfully deserves. Taking this extra step will also bring about more resolution in your life. The more you reach out and listen to those you've hurt in the past, the more possible it will feel to return to the person you once were before your LIB took over your life.

The problem with giving other people free rein to open up and reveal their pain is that they may attack you. That can be unhealthy for you because if the person isn't trying to be helpful and constructive, your wall may go back up to protect your feelings. Even though the person may have every right to be upset, he or she needs to speak to you from a place of honesty, not anger. If you feel that this person is beginning to lose their temper, just be completely honest and say:

"I'm here to make my amends and finally stop my behavior, but I'm afraid that, if I'm attacked, I may close down and not hear everything you have to say. I want to understand what my actions have done so I can avoid hurting anyone else like I've obviously hurt you. Can you help me by calmly telling me how I hurt you?"

Step 3. Understand that not everyone will accept your apology

Not every encounter you'll have will be what you hoped for. It's very likely that you'll approach some people who are simply not ready to forgive you for what your LIB did to them. Or you may find others who feel tongue-tied, trapped, or too nervous to talk.

If some people aren't receptive to your apology, don't be angry or upset, and don't push the issue any further. Remember, you're catching them off-guard with a conversation they never expected to be having. They may not even remember all the pain your LIB has caused them and may need time to feel comfortable enough to address it. If this happens, simply run through these five points in the following order, knowing that even the person who's not ready to accept your apology can be A NAIL in your recovery:

1. AGREE with their decision and let them know you entirely understand.

2. NOTIFY them of every negative action you're aware of, and then apologize for each one.

3. APOLOGIZE for the things you may not know about.

4. INVITE them to discuss their feelings anytime, if they ever want to.

5. LET them know that you plan to stay on top of your problem.

You might say something like, "I completely understand that you aren't in that place right now, and I know this is a lot to put on you unexpectedly. I just wanted to tell you how deeply sorry I am for any problems my past behaviors may have caused you, especially when I [insert any actions you're aware of here]. And if there are other ways I've hurt you that I'm not aware of, I truly apologize for those as well. If you ever feel comfortable enough to speak to me so I can truly understand the pain I've caused you and give you the apology you truly deserve, please feel free to reach me anytime. Until then, please know that I'm going to keep doing what I can to overcome my problem."

The end result of handling things this way may not feel as satisfying as receiving forgiveness from someone, but showing the right amount of effort, sincerity, and honesty still matters and turns that person into a nail. Even though you might not have gotten what you hoped for initially, your efforts are still a testament to how serious you are about beating denial and your LIB.

Step 4. Ask if there is anyone you may have forgotten

Denial has a way of hiding not just our LIB but some of the people it may have hurt along the way. You may be oblivious to how many people your LIB has affected because some individuals may have quietly removed themselves from your life.

Once you've apologized to a person on your list for everything you've done, ask if he or she can think of anyone else you may be forgetting about who deserves amends. You can even show the individual your list of people to apologize to, if you feel comfortable doing so. Not only does this show how sincere you are in beating your LIB, but learning that they weren't alone in being hurt by your LIB may even make the people you apologize to feel better.

LISTEN, THEN WRITE

As people open up about how your LIB hurt them, add those experiences to your letter from chapter 12 and then let each person know you're doing so. When you write down experiences you weren't aware of in your letter to yourself, the impact on both of you can be powerful. That act on your part—letting them know you've made their experience a part of something you plan to use every day to remind yourself never to be that person again—makes a strong statement to others that their pain matters to you.

SUGGESTION 6: DIVIDE YOUR LIFE UP THE RIGHT WAY

Now that the seven-day denial audit has shown you how you divide up your typical week, it's time to rebalance your books, so to speak.

Getting Started

If your seven-day denial audit helped you discover your LIB, then you're already aware of how you're spending your time. You also have a much clearer sense of how much time you devote to behaviors that are healthy versus those that are not. It's these numbers that you can now use to divide your time the right way in order to reset your life and bring it into a better state of balance. Using these numbers as your guide, you need to recalculate the amount of time you spend doing certain things each day, depending on your LIB.

Here are the changes necessary to shift your life back into a better state of balance.

Find what's unhealthy—then replace it with the exact opposite

Certain LIBs—especially severe LIBs—are simply unacceptable, no matter how little time you spend doing them according to your seven-day audit. Allowing yourself to be abused, being abusive, suffering from or ignoring any health or psychological issues, or continuing to do any LIB that endangers your life or the life of someone else is no longer an option. However, you can't just replace your LIB with some random activity, because chances are that you might simply substitute another LIB.

Instead, whenever you get the urge to engage in your LIB, I want you to spend that time doing something that's the exact opposite of your LIB:

- If it's ignoring a situation, then face it head-on.

- If it's engaging in a negative emotion, such as greed, maliciousness, or jealousy, try generosity, kindness, and being complimentary instead.

- If it's eating, drinking, or taking something unhealthy, then do something healthy for yourself.

- If it's being fearful of something, ask someone within your circle of trust to help you overcome it.

If there's no exact opposite behavior to your LIB, try engaging in activities that make you the least stressed and the most happy. Can't think of any? Then try scanning your seven-day denial audit for activities with no letters written next to them. These are the types of activities that you probably don't allow yourself to enjoy as often as you should. Instead of limiting yourself to the amount of time you spent on them during your seven-day denial audit, try spending the amount of time you would normally waste on your LIB on these activities instead.

Find out what's acceptable—then stick to those numbers

Some LIBs are trickier than others to simply replace with positive behaviors, since some LIBs may be healthy when done in moderation. For example,

- If your LIB is addiction to technology, I couldn't ask you to never use your cell phone or answer another e-mail.

- If your LIB is obsession about cleaning, I couldn't tell you to stop cleaning your house or you would eventually live in filth.

- If your LIB is being a shopaholic, I couldn't tell you to never make another purchase or you would never be independent.

- If your LIB is exercise bulimia, I couldn't tell you never to work out again or you would miss out on all the health benefits.

What you need to do is set realistic time limits on any activities that, done to excess, become LIBs in your life. That way, you'll know what's considered normal behavior and be able to moderate an otherwise healthy activity before it turns into a LIB. The statistics from chapter 9 tell you the average amount of time people typically spend doing certain activities. You can use this information as a guide, but your LIB may not be on that list. In that case, finding a specialist in the area of your LIB can help.

Asking an expert to advise you on what is considered the normal amount of time, energy, or money that should be spent on certain activities can help you understand the new limitations you need to set for yourself. If possible, consider hiring someone to do your LIB for you, then watch how long it typically takes them.

For example,

- For people I've known whose LIB was texting, e-mailing, or excessive Web surfing, I've suggested that they hire a time management specialist or a temporary administrative assistant to instruct them on the proper amount of time they should be spending on handling these day-to-day needs.

- For people whose LIB is obsessive cleaning, I've suggested hiring a house cleaner, then timing the cleaner from start to finish so they can see how many hours it really takes to clean their house from top to bottom.

- For people whose LIB is excessive shopping, I've had them ask a money manager to set up the best budget and allowance to enable them to stay within their financial means.

- For people whose LIB is over-exercising, I've recommended hiring a personal trainer for an hour to give them an idea of how many hours they really need to invest in exercise to stay fit and healthy.

Once you know exactly how long your LIB should take you to do, stick to that amount of time—no matter what. Here are a couple of tricks that can help you keep your promise:

- Call someone in your circle of trust as soon as you start any activity that's a LIB, then have them call you back once the average amount of time runs out.

- Invest in a stopwatch or timer that rings after a set period of time.

SLOW OR FAST—WHAT'S THE BEST APPROACH?

Should you ease your way into a more balanced life or immediately reorganize every aspect of your life? That depends on your LIB. The real recovery from severe LIBs comes from surrendering immediately and making changes in your life uncompromisingly. There is no way to slowly pull back on a severe LIB, because even the smallest amount of time spent on it could be lethal.

In the case of passive LIBs, however, or aggressive LIBs that may not seem to present an urgent problem, you might think that these changes can be introduced at your leisure. That's where you would be wrong. To end any LIB, you still need to organize your life without delay. Trying to slowly wean yourself off your LIB gives you more flexibility to try to control or manipulate it. When you try to change your behaviors at a slower pace, it also means that you don't believe in every fiber of your being that your LIB is a serious issue.

The single most effective way to remove a LIB from your life is to take it as seriously as if it were a severe LIB. That means that whether your LIB is using crystal meth or using your phone to text incessantly, you need to stop your old ways immediately and relearn a new way of living. If, for some reason, you can't do that right away, then taking smaller steps to start is better than doing nothing at all. I would rather watch you give up small portions of control in your life than give up none. Both paths—the path of immediate, uncompromising change and the path of small incremental steps—will get you there, so long as you stay on the path. Ultimately, however, treating your LIB as if it could be fatal will decrease your chances of failure.

Find a friend from your circle of trust—then be open to suggestion

Volunteer to give up a few hours of your week—hours you would typically spend on your LIB—and ask members of your circle of trust how they would like to see you spend that time. Find out from them if there are any other ways you could balance your time better, then be prepared to not just listen to and consider their requests, but put yourself out there by agreeing to try their requests, no matter what they are. The people who genuinely love you almost always know what holes in your life need to be filled.

I won't lie to you: it won't be comfortable at first surrendering these hours and giving up control. It's hard to accept that someone else is making a decision that may be the opposite of what you want and of how you expect things to be done. But if you can learn to accept their suggestions and implement them—starting in small doses, then gradually adding more time to the equation—then that's where the healing process starts.

That's because releasing your life into the hands of others who care about you can make you start feeling more comfortable about letting go of other things, especially your LIB. It also helps ensure that you'll be experiencing a variety of different, unique, and healthy activities throughout your week. Who knows? You may find that your next dream to chase may not be a forgotten one from days past, but a new one introduced by a friend.

15

Keeping the Wall Down for Good

Your wall of denial is finally down, but for some people, that doesn't mean that denial and their LIB are gone forever.

When people break free of denial for the first time and take control of their LIB, many float on what recovery experts call the "pink cloud." Suddenly everything feels perfect in their life because their life is finally running more smoothly. It's a sensation that leaves most deniers feeling euphoric and even childlike, but the reality is that the pink cloud eventually starts to dissipate, which is when reality finally comes crashing back in at them from all sides.

The best way I can explain it to my clients is to compare the pink cloud to that feeling you get when you take a nice long vacation. It's much easier to escape all of your stresses and worries when you have many positive distractions happening around you. You feel removed from the rest of the world—until that last day of vacation when your brain begins to remember all of the work, issues, people, and negative situations that await you at home.

Unfortunately for some people, the satisfaction that comes with breaking down their denial is only a temporary experience. Beating denial is a lot like getting in the best shape of your life: if you suddenly stop exercising and eating right, can you honestly expect to stay in that kind of shape forever? Remaining fit and healthy takes work, even if the effort isn't as difficult as it was in the beginning. In the same way, staying free of denial requires that you regularly look over a daily checklist of things that help keep denial from finding a way back into your life. That's why deniers who have beaten severe LIBs such as alcohol or drug addiction know exactly how many days, weeks, months, or years it's been since they conquered their LIB: they know it's work, and they also know that every missed meeting, every excuse, every little misstep is a brick that begins to build the wall of denial right back up.

I know you may feel successful today, but you can't ignore the fact that your success could instantly change tomorrow. That's why it's best to take a look at your denial every day and in the same way, no matter how insignificant your LIB may seem or how confident you are that it's never coming back. Just as quickly as this book has helped bring your wall down, the wall can rise back up. From this point forward, it's all about being one step ahead of your denial and continuing to do the work. I know, not only because I see how quickly my clients leap back into denial when they stop, but because I live it too.

To this day, I almost don't believe I have an addiction problem because it's been so many years since I stopped. Surprisingly, I no longer even crave the same things I once did. I don't miss them. But the only reason I feel this way is that I've never stopped doing the work it takes to stay one step ahead of my LIBs. I've seen so many people stop doing the work, then watched as denial slowly came back into their lives, erasing everything they had achieved up until that point.

There are going to be times in your life that are harder than others. There will be times when you want desperately to jump back into your old ways. The key is learning how to minimize how often you experience those bad times and understanding how to handle them when they're simply unavoidable. If you're afraid your LIB may be too strong to keep it away forever, here are the most effective tools you can try to keep you from rebuilding your wall, so that you never have to stop living the healthy life you want and deserve.

HOW TO MINIMIZE THE BAD TIMES

Follow the Fifteen–Fifteen Rule

Have you ever heard a song that instantaneously changed your mood from negative to positive? Have you ever experienced music that spontaneously changed your entire disposition from feeling bad to feeling relaxed, happy, or energized?

Meditation, when done properly, can evoke an immediate change in how you feel, transforming all of your stressful thoughts and painful urges into peaceful ones and shifting your thinking away from your LIB. That's why every morning, when I wake up, I meditate. Before every intervention I do for a family, I meditate. Whenever I have a moment during the day when I feel my thoughts are overwhelming my actions, I meditate.

Getting in fifteen minutes of meditation first thing in the morning and fifteen minutes of meditation at night is ideal for keeping our LIBs in check because meditation quells the worries, tensions, and negative feelings that usually trigger our LIBs in the time in between.

If you think you don't have that much time to spend, then think about how many times you hit the snooze bar when you first wake up in the morning. If you usually hit it twice, that's more than fifteen minutes right there. Now think about how long it takes you to fall asleep. Do you usually lie awake before finally drifting off to sleep with thoughts racing through your brain? In that same space of time, you could be meditating and releasing a lot of the worries and tensions that are preventing you from falling asleep right away.

If you simply don't have that much time to devote to meditation, then do it for at least five minutes whenever you feel the pull of your

LIB building up inside you. That small amount of time can still have a huge effect and bring your mood back on track in a positive way that will prevent you from relying on a LIB. (For a full explanation of how to meditate, see chapter 16.)

Find Others Like Yourself

Have you ever spoken to someone who really seems to get you?

Sometimes it's hard to take advice from someone who you feel has never walked a mile in your shoes. After all, how can you completely accept a person's opinions if you feel that he or she honestly doesn't understand the thoughts, feelings, and challenges you experience with your LIB? It's like taking business advice from someone who has never run a business or marriage advice from someone who has never walked down the aisle. It just doesn't feel reliable, even if it's solid advice.

The people in your circle of trust—your friends, your family, and your peers—may all be coming from a place of love, but they may not all be coming from a place of understanding, especially if they've never personally dealt with your type of denial or LIB. Even though I encouraged you to pick a few people for your circle of trust who share your LIB, it's possible that you were unable to enlist any. But that doesn't mean you shouldn't try to seek out others like yourself outside of your circle of trust. Regardless of the mildness or severity of your LIB, finding others who are experiencing the same urges, problems, and situations as you is incredibly helpful in keeping yourself in check.

The best advice typically comes from those who know our worlds and share our problems. That's why most drug, alcohol, and addiction counselors and interventionists who handle severe LIBs are recovering deniers themselves—just like me. Listening to someone who shares your LIB and has kept it in check makes you feel that this person's opinions are coming from a place of complete and total understanding. Such a person also provides substantial and living proof that it is possible to stay out of denial and keep your LIB at bay.

Another reason to find others like yourself is that it may be much easier to discuss certain topics and issues with them that you may not feel comfortable discussing with those in your circle of trust. With my clients, I compare it to what it's like for war veterans who have a difficult time talking about their experiences in combat with those who have never been to war. When asked about what happened to them in battle by someone who's never been there, they may never say a word. Yet two veterans from the same war who find themselves in a room together are likely to openly discuss the bloodiest of details. That's because both of them know that they're speaking to someone who's been in their shoes. They don't feel judged, ashamed, or reticent about certain feelings that may be preventing their true opinions, feelings, and emotions from coming out.

Finding someone like yourself also forces you to be accountable and gives you someone for whom you need to stay strong. Sometimes we do things for others that we're not willing to do for ourselves. Knowing that you're someone else's support can make you less likely to fall back into your LIB, especially if you feel as if you'll be closing out someone who needs your help as much as you need theirs.

Not sure where to find others like yourself? The good news (and I guess bad news, in a way) is that for every single LIB, there are millions of other people who have already traveled down the road you're on now. Depending on your LIB, the best place to start is to use the resources in chapter 18, talk with a doctor or therapist, or do a quick Internet search. There are support groups for nearly every aggressive and severe LIB that exists, many of which offer meetings in your area, as well as online support groups and conference call support groups. But you don't always have to turn to an official organization or expert to find deniers like yourself. You might bond with a neighbor who was abused in the same way you were, or a co-worker who shares the same emotional, psychological, or health issue you've been ignoring, or an old friend who is battling the same addiction you're now out of denial about.

Anyone will do, as long as it's someone you feel sufficiently relaxed around to really open up with and someone who has nothing to gain by redirecting you back into denial (for example, a co-worker who stands to benefit from revealing your secrets).

Do a Nightly Recount

Whatever the LIB you've overcome, it was nothing more than a temporary bandage that served to fill in the void you felt within yourself. With your wall of denial broken down and your LIB in check, you need some sort of daily reassurance that you're closing those voids for good. That's where a nightly recount comes in. Looking back on how you acted all day long holds you accountable for all your behaviors, both good and bad. With this kind of daily review, you'll immediately know if there are areas of your life that need improvement—and immediately see areas that may deserve praise.

Before you fall asleep each night, spend a few minutes doing a quick inventory of how you handled yourself throughout the entire day. Starting from the very first minute you rose out of bed, ask yourself:

- Did I conduct myself in a manner that I'm not proud of?

- Did I lie to or try to manipulate anyone?

- Do I owe anyone an apology?

- Did I say something that may have hurt someone's feelings?

- Did I lose my temper?

- Did I ignore someone who needed and deserved my attention?

- Was there something I could have done or handled better?

How you answer these simple questions lets you instantly evaluate whether you're still on top of the things that will keep your LIB from becoming a crutch again. If you answered yes to any of these questions, look at what that says about what you need to work on the next day or who you need to apologize to. Any no answers point to where you deserve to feel satisfied with yourself and can reinforce your positive, healthy behaviors the next day.

HOW TO HANDLE THE BAD TIMES WHEN THEY'RE UNAVOIDABLE

Nothing makes me prouder than knowing that you're in control of your denial, but being strong one day doesn't mean that life won't have a few surprises for you the next day.

There will be times when you are tempted by your LIB. If you were being abused, the person who abused you may try to come back into your life. If you were in denial about a bad habit or an addiction, there may be trying times that make you depressed, nervous, or anxious enough to crave your old ways. If you have a disorder or physical issue, there might be times when admitting your problem leaves you feeling broken or weak, which is when you could make the mistake of ignoring your physical issue in order to feel strong again.

The problems and situations that could trigger your LIB are simply inescapable, but that doesn't mean you can't ride through the bad times with ease. Here are some of the best ways to dodge the bullets that are aimed at sending you back into denial.

Look Ahead and Find the Potholes

If you spend less time worrying about an unavoidable situation in your life that's going to be uncomfortable for you and more time preparing for it, knowing that it's coming up gives you an advantage. At the start of each week, scan ahead—a week, a month, or even a year—to look for certain circumstances that you know will be difficult to deal with. That way, you can prepare for these difficult situations and ensure that you don't fall into any "potholes."

It could be a wedding where alcohol is being served or where you know you will be the only unmarried one in attendance. It could be a time of year when your job is more intense and your stress level runs higher than usual. It could be a business trip when you'll be away from those in your circle of trust. Regardless of your LIB, think ahead and ask yourself:

- Is there an event, holiday, or anniversary coming up that may make it challenging to keep my LIB in check?

- Is this the time of year when I feel more stress for a certain reason?

- Is there a trip I have to take that may make it easier to fall back into my LIB?

- Is there a block of time coming up when it may be impossible to reach anyone in my circle of trust?

Once you've looked far enough ahead to see dates and times that may be difficult to handle, start planning your counteroffensive by making sure you'll be doing something positive on those days as well. Try to arrange your schedule so that someone in your circle of trust is either with you during that time or easily reachable. However, don't ask someone who shares your LIB to stay with you. The situation may be equally tempting, difficult, or stressful for that person as it is for you.

Once you have a game plan, you'll feel far less stressed in the days leading up to the pothole. In fact, you may discover that you don't even need to rely on your backup person when you finally reach the pothole. Many times, just knowing that someone is there for you and understands that you're being challenged feels comforting enough to keep you in balance.

Talk It Through with Those Who Care About You

As the days leading up to a denial-challenging event or situation tick away, begin speaking about it with every person in your circle of trust, as well as with any others you've found who share your LIB. Even though you may feel you can overcome the challenge that awaits you, it's always empowering to hear the same thing being said by those who care about you.

Don't feel bad asking for advice or support. Those closest to you have most likely begun to wonder how you'll handle the upcoming pothole, even before you've turned to them for help. Trust me when I say that they will be relieved to know that you're addressing the pothole and will far prefer giving you the help you're asking for over anxiously wondering whether you're going to relapse into your old behaviors. By speaking to each person in your circle about the challenge ahead, not only will you feel more motivated to stay on-track, but you'll also be making yourself—and those in your circle of trust—feel more relaxed.

Play the Tape Through

It only takes one slipup to be thrust back into denial. You need to remind yourself that one simple, seemingly harmless action led to major problems in your past, and it can happen again. Remember just how unfulfilling the LIB was in the end. Remind yourself that, by jumping off-track, you risk having that same experience happen again—only this time you may end up in even worse shape than before.

When I work with individuals who suffer from severe LIBs—drug addiction, alcoholism, eating disorders—I use (as do many top professionals) a proven technique called "playing the tape through." I ask my clients to think about the worst thing that happened as a result of their LIB, from start to finish, to remind them of the reasons why they shouldn't succumb to their old life-imbalancing habits. I ask them to recall not only the worst experience from their past but one in which they thought they were in control of their LIB but ended up suffering a tragic outcome. This is the "tape" I have them use whenever they feel tempted to fall back into their LIB. Before they take that first misstep, I ask them to play the tape through in their minds from start to finish. For example:

- If you were being abused, it might be remembering the time you risked going back to your spouse after he apologized and claimed he had changed, then ended up hospitalized and in a shelter a few weeks later.

- If you were in denial of a psychological disorder, it could be remembering the time you thought you were better and opted to stop taking your medication, then had your condition run out of control, costing you your job, a close friend, or something else you valued but could never get back.

- If you're an alcoholic about to take a drink, it might be remembering the time you had one drink just to fit into the crowd, and then found yourself in jail, not remembering a thing about how you ended up there but hearing horrible stories from your friends and family about how you acted that night.

- If you're a gambler about to make just one bet on a "sure thing," it could mean remembering the time you felt safe placing a simple twenty-dollar bet, then ended up losing your savings, missing your rent payment, and being evicted.

- If you're in denial of a physical issue, it might be remembering the time you ignored the warning signs of a different health problem, then found yourself rushed to the emergency room.

- If you were in denial of being in debt, it could be remembering the time you skipped a few payments, then had something repossessed—or, worse, had to file for bankruptcy.

If you've been fortunate enough up to this point to not have a horror story attached to your LIB, that's fine. The tape you play through at tempting times doesn't have to be something that's already happened to you. What I do with some clients is to ask, "What's the absolute worst-case scenario if your LIB runs out of control once more?" Some have told me that it would be losing a certain friendship. Others have said it would be having to work three jobs to pay off their bills. I've heard every worst-case scenario, from losing your dignity, integrity, or pride to going bankrupt, suffering a mental breakdown, being abandoned by everyone you love, and even death.

Run through as many scenarios as possible and pick the single worst thing that could happen to you. Then, whenever you feel the urge to fall back on your LIB, "play the tape through" before taking another step.

Remind . . . with a Rewind

I sometimes feel that the addicts who've been treated on my show are lucky. They're lucky not just because they have finally been able to get help for their problems, but because the show provides them with a recorded account of their LIB and the damage it caused in their life. They have a DVD they can pop in whenever they feel tempted by their LIB to remind them exactly how imbalanced their life was before they broke free of denial.

There's nothing preventing you from doing something similar. Try recording a video of yourself at a positive moment when you feel happy, content, and proud of your actions. Because you already own your denial on paper and have a contract with someone from your circle of trust, I won't offer a specific formula for what you could say to yourself in this recording, but it should do three things:

1. It should remind you of another time when you were tempted by your LIB but felt strong enough to walk away.

2. It should remind you that you're strong enough to do that again.

3. It should accomplish this in three to five minutes. When viewing this video, you could be seconds away from temptation. Keeping your message short will prevent it from taking too long to motivate you. A short video can deliver a quick and powerful positive boost when you need it most.

Make Avoidance Your Last Option

Your first instinct when facing an upcoming challenge may be to avoid it altogether. After all, it's far easier to run from a problem than it is to face it. But think about it: running away from a problem is what you were doing the entire time you spent in denial. Now that your wall is down, you've already stood your ground against what's been throwing your life off-balance and you've won. Yes, these new challenges may be difficult, but they're still nothing compared to how far you've already come.

The tools I recommend here can help you get through the upcoming challenge unscathed, but if you can't get the extra support you need for some reason—perhaps because of conflicting schedules—then your best option may be to walk away from the situation. Before you do, I recommend speaking to everyone in your circle of trust one more time and letting each of them know what you're planning to do. Odds are that you have not impressed upon them enough how difficult the pothole you're about to face will be for you. I can guarantee with almost absolute certainty that there will be at least one person in your circle of trust who finds the time to be available to you.

16

Silence Your Mind with Meditation

Before I came to where I am now, I struggled with my own demons. After recovering from my battles with several severe LIBs (drug dependency and alcoholism) and remaining clean for twelve years, I was expecting more from my life. I thought I would be happier, yet there was a dark cloud of depression that would always surface and cling to me when I least expected it.

My therapist at the time would constantly remind me to meditate; but, to be honest, meditation was one part of my treatment program that I never bothered to do on a regular basis, if at all. When my depression got to the point where it almost literally consumed me, I purchased a gun on the Internet with the intention of ending my life once it arrived. In the middle of waiting for the gun to be delivered, I broke down and told my therapist that I thought I needed to be on something to ease my depression. Reluctant to have me turn to drugs to battle my despair, he begged me one last time to set aside a single hour each day to meditate, for one straight week. Frustrated with his badgering on the subject, I decided I would finally take his advice, just to prove to him that it didn't work. I wanted him to know that meditation couldn't help what I felt inside myself. So each day for a week I turned off the phones, set a timer, and spent an hour in silence.

I committed myself 150 percent to it, because I knew that if I didn't give meditation my complete and undivided attention, it was my last chance.

That week, the anxiety I had always suffered from, and that feeling I always had of being uncomfortable in my own skin, slowly lifted. Up until that point, I had always looked outward to other things for an escape or relief, yet meditation had given me a strange sense of inner comfort and peace I had never experienced before.

With each day, I found the negative things in my life became less magnified, while the positive things in my life finally started to come into focus. I finally stopped listening to the tape that always played inside me—the tape that told me I wasn't any good and that I didn't deserve happiness. Suddenly, the volume of that tape began to lower itself and I could finally concentrate on my place in the universe. It was always there, but it wasn't until I tapped into meditation that I began to develop a sense of how I could better my life—and the world around me—one day at a time.

One week later, the gun arrived, but I didn't need it. Staying dedicated to meditation had helped me develop a renewed sense of purpose and a complete sense of self, and because of that, I finally felt at peace.

The dark cloud of depression I always felt hanging over me was suddenly lifted. And for me, someone who had carried some form of depression for his entire life, that feeling was nothing short of a miracle. I finally understood the power of meditation and realized at that moment that having faith in it is when true miracles can happen. That was seven years ago, and to this day, I have not taken a single antidepressant nor have I been depressed.

I'm telling you my story to let you know that, if you think meditation isn't for you, I understand completely. But forget about the mystical and spiritual aspects of meditation that may make you apprehensive about trying it. Forget the fact that it is beneficial to your body and mind for numerous reasons, including its ability to lower blood pressure and anxiety, lower cholesterol and the levels of the stress hormone cortisol in your body, boost your immune system, and even inspire you to think more creatively. There's actually a specific reason why meditation is crucial for deniers like myself, my clients, and now you.

You see, the most common problem that deniers suffer from is having a mind that doesn't want to stop. Regardless of how relaxed they may be with other objectives and priorities, all deniers—especially those with aggressive or severe LIBs—tend to have brains that can never turn off the thoughts and emotions that revolve around, or contribute to, their LIB. Making an effort to ease their minds can quell their negative thoughts and emotions and turn them neutral or positive before they grow into negative urges and actions.

THE BASICS: SET, SIT, SHUT, AND STICK

SET the right atmosphere

First, pick a quiet spot where you can be sure you won't be disturbed for fifteen minutes. This should be a place that is absolutely free of all distractions. If that means locking the door, unplugging or turning off your phone, and telling others not to disturb you, then by all means, do so.

You may find it difficult to find such a peaceful spot, and that's one of the reasons I encourage meditating first thing in the morning and right before bed. Those times tend to be the least dramatic and most tranquil moments of the day. The more you practice meditation, the less necessary it'll be for you to be this quiet to achieve the same stress-relieving effects.

SIT in a comfortable position

Get into a relaxing seated position, but don't lie down; you don't want to find yourself drifting off to sleep instead of meditating. A chair is fine (as long as it doesn't recline), or you can sit on a cushion on the floor with your back flat against the wall. You can bring your feet together, cross your legs, or tuck your heels under your butt—whichever position feels best to you. As long as your spine is straight and you're in a position that's not so relaxing that you get sleepy, you'll be fine.

Once you're in a position you like, feel free to wedge a few pillows under yourself to get as comfortable as possible. If anything feels achy or difficult, adjust yourself so that you're not distracted by the discomfort later on. Finally, relax your arms and rest your palms on your thighs.

SHUT your eyes

To tune out everything, you need to turn off everything, which is why closing your eyes is a must. However, even though they're to remain closed, remember to keep your eyes looking up as you meditate, as if you were looking forward. Some people droop their heads down as they start to relax. The lower your head dips, however, the more likely you are to fall asleep. Keeping your head upright, as if you were staring straight ahead, will ensure that you stay alert enough to concentrate on what you're meditating about—and not counting sheep instead.

STICK with it

The more frequently you practice meditation, the faster you'll be able to get yourself in a relaxed, calmer state of mind. You'll also be able to meditate for much longer periods of time than just fifteen minutes at a clip. After you attain both of these benefits, you'll be able to pacify your urges for your LIB almost instantly, no matter how long those urges last.

FOUR SIMPLE WAYS TO MEDITATE

Truth be told, I don't really believe in one set form of meditation. What works best to slow down the racing mind of one denier may not be as productive for another denier. I had one client in particular who was completely anxious trying to meditate in complete silence yet felt entirely stress-free once she began chanting her child's name over and over again. For her, it was soothing to focus on someone who meant something to her. That's why I think it's important to find the right form of meditation that works best for you.

Once you've set the right atmosphere, sat yourself down, and shut your eyes, you need to choose something to focus on. Here are the top four easiest—and most effective—things you can choose. Each time you meditate, pick one and stick with it for a week before moving on to the next one. Once you've tried all four, decide which one left you feeling most relaxed, then continue to use it.

1. Your Breathing

Begin breathing in through your nose as slowly and as deeply as you can. Hold your breath for one to two seconds, then slowly exhale out through your mouth. As you inhale, try not to let your chest rise, but let your stomach expand instead—your breaths will be much deeper, and you'll take in more oxygen. As you exhale, try to force your lungs to empty by gently pushing out as much air as you can. Pause, then slowly begin to inhale once again.

With each breath, try focusing on the air as it flows in through your nose and out through your mouth. Here are some tricks to help you clear your head:

- Focus on your inhalations for a few breaths, then focus for a few breaths on holding your breath, then focus on your exhalations for a few more breaths, then finish by focusing on your exhalations to empty your lungs. Repeat the cycle.

- Don't count your breaths—just concentrate on what you're feeling as air enters your nostrils, how your lungs feel as you hold in your breath, and how your lips feel as each breath leaves your mouth.

- Try placing your hand over your belly to give you another thing to focus on. Concentrate on your belly as it rises and descends with each and every breath.

2. A Thought or Object

Instead of letting your mind race with random thoughts, give it one specific thought to chew on. The thought shouldn't be a problem, an issue, a memory, or anything that will drum up emotions and other thoughts, but a simple thought or object that you can picture in your mind and concentrate on.

If you choose a thought, try to make it one word that symbolizes something positive, such as peace, hope, or love. If you choose an object, make it something simple and serene, or something that makes you feel good, such as a flower, a waterfall, or a blue sky. As you continue to meditate and your mind begins to wander, refocus on that thought or object to help clear your mind once more.

3. Your Body

Start by focusing on the toes of your left foot for a few deep breaths. Then begin to work your way up the left side of your body, focusing on each part of your body for another few deep breaths, until you reach your head. For example, after focusing on your toes, move on to your foot, then your ankle, shin, knee, thigh, hips, chest, shoulders, neck, face, and hair. Once you've reached the top, reverse the order and descend down the right side of your body until you reach the toes on your right foot.

Next, work your way back up your body, only this time focus on body parts that are behind you, travel up through your body, then into your arms. For example, after focusing on the toes of your right foot, move onward to your heel, your calf, the inside of your knee, thigh, butt, lower back, shoulder blades, upper arms, elbows, forearms, wrist, palm, and each finger. Then reverse the order by going back up in your shoulders, across into your left arm, then back down your body until you end up right back where you started—focusing on the toes of your left foot.

4. A Mantra

Some people prefer to prevent their mind from drifting by thinking about or saying a specific word or short phrase, then repeating it over and over and over again, either aloud or in their head. Any word or phrase that works for you will do, but it should be something that's easy to say and doesn't stir up any negative thoughts or feelings. (Your ex-spouse's first name may not be the best choice, for example.)

The mantra I personally use is "Om Namah Shivaya," which means, "I bow to my inner self." If you're uncertain what mantra to use, these suggestions may help:

- Pick a sound that doesn't make any sense but easily rolls off your tongue or is easy to hum.

- Have someone you care about choose a word, which might have more meaning for you than something you pick yourself.

- Go on the Internet and do a search for popular mantras. Depending on which style of meditation you find, many mantras have special meanings, so you may find one that relates perfectly to you.

- Stick with the classic "Om." It's not only easy to say but timeless as well.

Regardless of which type of meditation you choose, the mantra you whisper to yourself, or the kind of thing you decide to focus on, the best piece of advice I can offer is to just listen to and trust your instincts. Don't be afraid to try all of the options I've offered in this chapter before deciding which one leaves you feeling the most relaxed, energized, and focused. Your body and mind will let you know when you've found what works best for you.

17

When It's Not You in Denial

So what do you do if the only denial left in your life is actually someone else's denial? After all, if everyone is in denial about something, then one thing is certain: you probably know someone who also suffers from a LIB. For example, do you

- Know your best friend is in denial about being in an abusive relationship?

- Feel helpless watching your spouse fall into a depressive state that he or she won't admit to?

- Have a relative who you know is withering away from an eating disorder that he or she pretends doesn't exist?

- Have parents who can no longer take care of themselves yet refuse to believe they need professional care?

- Fear for a friend who's sliding deeper and deeper into financial debt but can't seem to see all the obvious signs?

When you know about someone else's denial yet refuse to do anything about it, then guess what? You're still in denial, even if you already have a handle on your own LIB. The only difference is that, instead of ignoring a problem in your own life, you're ignoring a problem in someone else's life—someone who may desperately need your help.

You might feel awkward about getting involved or worry that speaking up would be impolite. Or maybe you're not as concerned about other people's issues, since you have your own to contend with. But the fact is that, even if you're not a take-charge type or a caring type, someone else's out-of-balance life has a way of spilling over into yours. In short: when those closest to you are imbalanced, it causes some imbalance in your own life. Just as your own LIB indirectly hurts the people who care about you, their LIB has the same hurtful effect on you, whether you realize it or not. By helping someone bring balance back into their life, you're actually making it easier to keep yours in balance as well.

There are two ways to help other people whose lives are out of balance. You can get them their own copy of this book, which will allow them to spot their own denial and LIB, just as you've been able to do. Or you can use the tools in the next two chapters if you feel that they may not be interested enough to read this book or that they may need immediate help with their LIB. Either way, I can show you how to break down their wall of denial so that they get the help they need, while you bring even more balance to your life.

SETTING UP YOUR OWN CONCERNED SIT-DOWN

If everyone you care about came to you and warned that something was wrong with your car, would you grab the keys and risk driving it or would you immediately look under the hood? You already know what your answer would be. After all, if everyone who cares about you takes the time to come together as a group to deal with a problem that concerns all of them simultaneously, then there must be a problem, right?

So ask yourself this: what if those same people had come together and approached you about your LIB and asked you to do something about it? Because this book has helped you address your LIB, you may never know what your initial reaction might have been. But I can tell you this much: their intervention would have made it impossible for you to hide behind your denial any longer, and it would have made you feel loved enough to want to do something about it.

On the A&E show *Intervention,* that's exactly what I do to help break hard-core addicts—those who suffer from the most severe LIBs—out of denial. By surrounding addicts with their loved ones and the right tools, I've had the pleasure of taking deniers who are literally steps away from death's door and turning their lives around. By rounding up the right people, knowing what to expect, and staging what I like to call a "concerned sit-down," you can have the same life-changing result with someone you're worried about.

As you read through my instructions for setting up your own concerned sit-down, certain tips may be familiar to you, either from my show or from what you've read or heard about. What I'm about to share with you are modified versions of what I and other top interventionists use to break the cycle of denial in hard-core addicts. If the person you're thinking about suffers from a passive or aggressive LIB, you may think this approach is a bit over the top, but that's where you would be wrong. This approach is exactly what you need to do if you want to break someone of denial, regardless of how serious their LIB may be.

The fact is that using this technique has been shown to be the quickest and most effective way to get deniers to realize their situation so that they can begin addressing their LIB and bringing their life into a better state of balance. Straying too far from this method would be like building a new road to get somewhere important when there's already a road that runs straight to it. However, there is a way to tailor these steps a bit: the more passive the denier's LIB, the fewer steps you need to use.

Here's what you need to do to have a concerned sit-down for someone you care about.

Before You Begin

Although I'm about to offer you some great suggestions to start the process of a concerned sit-down, don't overlook the possibility of having some type of mediator present to run it instead. People have come up to me in airports, hotels, and other public places to tell me that, after watching my show, they've been moved to hold their own intervention on a loved one. I love seeing and feeling their desire to help, but if you can't communicate with the person in denial in the right way, the whole process—no matter how carefully you use the tools I'm about to share—could backfire and make things even worse.

That's why having someone who specializes in interventions present is always my first choice. A certified interventionist like myself is trained to constantly read the entire room (and the denier) and to handle and diffuse any possible conflict or situation. If you don't have the money or resources to hire an interventionist, or you feel that the denier's LIB isn't severe enough to warrant an interventionist, then the next best choice is someone who isn't affected by the denier's LIB and can see the situation in a different light, such as a counselor, social worker, private therapist, or minister, deacon, or some other clergyperson. Once you have your moderator, you can pass these tips on to them so they know what you're hoping to achieve.

Step 1: Setting Up the Sit-Down

Plan it like a surprise party

It's crucial to keep the event a secret from the denier. If that person catches wind of what you're planning to do, he or she will come up with a variety of different excuses for avoiding any invitation that seems even remotely suspicious. Make it clear to all participants that they are not to allude to the sit-down, even if they are confronted by the denier prior to the event.

Invite as many people as possible

There's an old expression: "If it walks like a duck and talks like a duck, it's a duck." If you can pull together twenty-five people who love the denier and will tell that person, "You're a duck," it becomes that much harder for the denier to stay in denial.

My favorite interventions are the ones that have at least twenty-five people present, because the size of the gathering shows the person in denial that there really is a problem. The more people you can get to surround the denier on that day—not just with their concern and love but also with the facts—the harder it is for the denier to manipulate the situation to try to avoid facing it. Such interventions truly force deniers to take a serious look at their problem, for what very well may be the first time in their life.

If it's impossible for you to draw that many people together, that's entirely fine; your sit-down will not necessarily be any less effective, as long as you've tried to round up as many people as you can who (1) *care* about the denier and (2) are *aware* of the denier's LIB. Don't just pull in people to fill seats—everyone present has to be someone who has been affected by the denier's LIB in order for their voice to make a difference.

If there's anyone who can't attend, whether because of prior commitments or geographic distance, try to pull that person on board via speakerphone, through an e-mail to be read aloud, or even with a video. Deniers need to see that it's not just the one or two people who always nag them who are concerned, but that a great many people in their life, if not all of them, are concerned about their well-being.

Invite as few people as possible when it's called for

If you're dealing with a denier whose LIB is one whose exposure might create more problems for the denier (or someone else) if it became widely known—such as sexual addiction, porn addiction, or denial about a child being gay who isn't completely out of the closet to others yet—then gathering a lot of people for a sit-down might cause more harm than good.

In this situation, instead of asking as many people as possible to participate, invite only the individuals who have been most severely affected by the denier's LIB—and who know all the facts—to attend the sit-down. For example, I once worked with a dad who was in denial about ignoring his son because he was gay. Not only was his LIB putting a strain on his relationship with his son, but his attitude toward his son was affecting his relationships with other people—some of whom weren't aware that his son was gay. The only people invited to this sit-down were those who were aware of both the father's LIB and the son's homosexuality, since inviting others who didn't know the son's secret could have indirectly hurt him.

Wait for the right day

You might assume that the best approach is to step in as soon as possible or to approach deniers right before they succumb to their LIB. In reality, neither approach is the wisest one to use.

Planning a concerned sit-down for a time immediately before deniers are about to succumb to their LIB—such as speaking to an alcoholic right before a party, talking to a workaholic at the start of her week, or confronting someone in debt at the start of the month when he has money—is like trying to take a plateful of steaks away from a starving tiger. To the denier, the LIB is that plate of steaks, and trying to take it away at a moment when that person is the most vulnerable to succumbing to it only breeds anger and resentment. Infuriating or agitating the denier is a bad tactic that makes your sit-down much less effective.

Instead, it's much wiser to let the tiger gorge itself on the steaks. Once the tiger has overeaten—which is essentially what a denier with an out-of-control LIB does—it will immediately notice the negative effects of what it has done. It will feel the pain in its belly and regret being so obsessed with overindulging itself. That's the exact moment when you need to catch the denier.

The best time to set up a concerned sit-down is immediately after the denier's LIB has caused that person to have feelings that are impossible to deny. It might be the morning after a drinking binge, an eighteen-day work burst, or an all-nighter spent surfing the Web. You need to wait for the perfect time when the denier's actions have caused remorse and regret so that you confront the person at a point of feeling vulnerable.

To be honest, you may have to be patient: the right moment may take days, weeks, or even months to appear. But looking for that moment creates your best possible opportunity. It's virtually impossible for deniers to ignore the damage their LIBs are having in their life when they're actually feeling that damage when you approach them. Instead, when they can see and feel the ramifications of their actions, you leave them little choice but to be more receptive to everyone's concerns.

Pick the right time

Once you've found the right day for an intervention with an addict who suffers from the most severe kind of LIB, I encourage you to schedule it for first thing in the morning, immediately after breakfast, for two important reasons:

1. People are more alert and receptive at that time of day. If you can catch deniers in a refreshed state with some food already in their stomach, you're more likely to get a positive response from them than when they're hungry and tired.

2. By approaching deniers before their day begins, you're catching them before they stumble across any triggers that could raise their desire to use their LIB. The sooner you can catch them in the day, the less likely they are to be edgy or anxious.

Choose the right place

The more unfamiliar the place you choose to have your concerned sit-down, the more reserved and uncomfortable the denier may feel. It's best to have the intervention in the denier's own surroundings, instead of arranging for it to be held in another location. In a familiar environment, the denier will feel more comfortable and better able to listen to you and everyone else involved.

The only way such an arrangement could backfire is if the denier is the only person on the lease or deed. Deniers who feel threatened enough and know their rights might pick up the phone, call the police, and have everyone thrown out. So you need to ask yourself if there's any chance that might happen before you decide to make the denier's home your sit-down spot. If such an outcome is a possibility, try holding the sit-down in the second-most comfortable place—typically the home of the person for whom the denier seems to have the most respect.

Bring plenty to eat

To keep everyone comfortable and less on edge, have enough food and drink available so that there's no excuse to bring the sit-down to an early close. You want the denier—and everyone else at the sit-down—to feel as settled and comfortable as possible. If you're bringing the denier to the sit-down spot, then stop for a meal on the way so the denier feels full on arrival.

Step 2: Writing the Letter

Each participant needs to prepare a short letter to read at the sit-down that addresses the denier's LIB. You might think this seems silly or even a little extreme, but writing and reading a letter has been shown to be 80 percent successful at instantly knocking down the wall of denial in people with severe LIBs. What's not as commonly understood is that reading a letter can be even more effective when used to handle other, less severe, types of LIBs, both passive and aggressive.

Hands down, every interventionist in the world would agree that the letter is the most valuable component of a sit-down. It's incredibly successful in getting the most stubborn deniers to recognize that they have a life that's horribly out of balance. The letter is often the impetus that encourages the denier to finally seek the help they so desperately need—that is, if it's written with all the right elements in place.

Here's how to construct the perfect letter so that you and every other person at your sit-down can have the same positive, life-balancing impact on the denier.

The Perfect Letter: Five Points

Before you start, keep in mind that nothing in your letter should come out of resentment, anger, or fear. Instead, before you write— and as you write—imagine that the denier is in the intensive care unit at a hospital and you are visiting and talking to the denier on his or her deathbed.

You see, no matter how upset you may be with someone's actions and behaviors, it's impossible to hold on to your anger when you experience the extreme sadness that arises when you realize that your time with them is short. To write a letter that will be the most effective in breaking the denial of the person for whom you're doing an intervention, you need to write from your heart. This trick can help place you in that mind-set. As you write each sentence, go back to imagining that you're losing this person forever. Depending on the denier's LIB, that may not be as difficult to imagine as you think.

Point 1

Start your letter by telling the denier why you're there with him or her that day. The most effective lines come from the heart. You might say, "Joe, I'm here today because I love and care about you," or, "Joe, I'm here today because I'm worried about you and your health." You need to begin by stating why you're present so that the denier instantly knows where you stand.

Point 2

Next, write down three positive experiences you've had with the denier that he or she will remember and relate to. If you want to relate a positive experience that the denier may not remember (such as a father telling his daughter about the day he brought her home from the hospital), that's fine, as long as your experience is one that expresses how much you love the denier.

Your description of each positive experience needs to be as detailed as possible because you want the denier to relate to it. You want to pick moments that will remind the denier of great moments when he or she felt happy, proud, accepted, or loved. You might also pick moments that made the denier feel connected to you emotionally, as an indirect reminder of how important you are in the denier's life. Reestablishing this connection will make the denier more receptive to the points you bring up later in the letter.

Also, if possible, choose experiences from before the time when the denier's LIB began to occur. Using such examples subtly connects these special moments to the time when the denier's life was still in balance. Your memory of experiences from this time offers proof that the denier once had control over his or her life in a way that evoked positive feelings. Your account of these experiences can bolster the fact that it's possible for the denier to achieve the same sense of comfort again and serves as a reminder that the denier was able to do amazing things when there was no LIB to contend with.

Point 3

Next, recall the first time you noticed the denier's LIB or realized this person had a problem. This time should be one of the first episodes you can think of that happened specifically between the denier and yourself.

It could be the first time you watched the denier avoid a phone call out of fear that it was a bill collector. Perhaps it was the first time you saw the denier looking out of breath from a health condition, or the time when you noticed how unnaturally skinny the denier seemed from not eating properly. Maybe it was the time you heard about the denier working all evening instead of being present to watch his or her child at a first dance recital.

Whatever instance you cite, be careful to write about it in a way that doesn't exhibit any anger or judgment. Describing how embarrassed or furious the denier's actions made you will only make that person shut down. Instead, talk about how the denier's actions made your heart feel. No matter how pissed off or mortified you may have been at that moment, there was still a part of you that felt helpless and sad for the denier. Recalling these emotions while explaining your first encounter with the denier's LIB is far more effective at conveying just how much you care. It also shows how the denier, consciously or not, is behaving in a way that negatively affects your life.

Point 4

Explain the three most devastating things that have occurred in your life as a result of the denier's LIB. These three examples may be either situations the denier is aware of or situations the denier may not even know about or remember being involved in. Maybe you lost an unhealthy amount of weight from worrying about the denier. Perhaps covering up for the denier's actions has cost you relationships with other people or taken a toll on your finances. Just be sure the three examples you choose are the three biggest disruptions in your life.

Again, as you list these negative consequences for you of the denier's actions, you need to stay in that same emotional place in your heart—free of any resentment or bitterness. The denier needs to understand that you're blaming the problem, not the person, and needs to hear about the damage caused by his or her actions, though not in a judgmental way.

By telling about how the denier's LIB, and not the denier personally, has affected you, you help to separate the individual from the

LIB so that the denier doesn't feel consumed with guilt. The denier is left feeling capable of choosing to prevent his or her LIB from hurting you. At the same time, hearing about these experiences of yours prevents the denier from adding more bricks to the wall of denial. Instead of attacking the denier, you're addressing his or her behaviors, and instead of judging, you're merely expressing how those behaviors made you feel.

Point 5

Once the denier understands that he or she has a problem that needs immediate attention, it's time to see if the denier is willing to consider getting help. End your letter by asking the denier directly to do something about their LIB and to give you an answer at that very moment.

Step 3: Conducting the Sit-Down

Bring your heart—not your anger

Each person at the sit-down needs to approach it in a nonjudgmental way. You don't want to attack the denier but instead to show concern about the denier's LIB. The goal of the sit-down isn't to judge but to make the denier aware of the problem and to give this person the tools to do something about it.

Expect to see the denier's wall of denial at its highest

Once deniers see everyone in one place for a meeting they were completely unaware of, their guard typically will go up immediately. Some deniers use their most aggressive tools to protect their LIB, including crying, throwing a tantrum, lying, and pretending to have a nervous breakdown. It's incredibly hard to see deniers at that moment of desperation, and you may feel guilty enough to want to turn back. Don't! That's exactly what these actions are trying to accomplish.

Instead, what you have to do is gently knock down the wall of denial. Allow the person you've chosen to run the sit-down to calmly speak with the denier and bring up the following three things:

1. Everyone present loves and cares for the denier very much.

2. Everyone present is concerned about the denier's health or state of mind (depending on the denier's LIB).

3. Everyone present has something they want to say to the denier personally.

Read each letter—in the right order

Once the denier has taken a seat next to whoever is running the sit-down, the moderator should ask each person to read their letter aloud. There are four approaches you can take when doing this:

1. You can start with the person the denier finds least threatening, then move on to the second least threatening person, and so on. Choosing the least threatening person has been proven to be much more effective in keeping deniers calmer, more receptive, and less confrontational—the ideal state of mind for getting through to them. Usually the least threatening person is the one to whom the denier might say, "Why are you even here?" When concern comes from someone the denier doesn't expect to see—either because that person has never voiced an opinion or because the person seems unlikely to have been affected by the denier's actions—it starts to hit home a lot faster, especially if that person has traveled a distance to be at the sit-

down. Maybe it's the denier's favorite uncle who lives on the opposite side of the country, or a close friend the denier sees only a few times a year. The point is that having the letter-reading started by a friend or relative the denier rarely sees can put a significant crack in the wall of denial.

2. You can start with the person you think would have the greatest impact on the denier, then move on to the second most significant person, and so on. When deniers are seconds away from exiting the sit-down, this may be the smarter method, since hearing first from those they care the most about may affect them enough to convince them to stay.

3. You can begin with those individuals who may not have the greatest impact, then move in order of importance so that you end the sit-down with a letter read by the most significant person. If you don't feel as much hesitation from the denier about staying, this can be a great strategy, since it lets you slowly build up the emotional intensity of the sit-down.

4. You can go around the room in no particular order of importance. If you choose this method, it may be helpful to start with whoever is sitting the farthest away from the denier, then gradually choose people sitting closer. Again, hearing each letter will be an emotional experience for the denier—the more closely people are sitting to the denier when they read, the more of an impact their letter may have.

Because everyone's letter should end by asking the denier to seek some form of help, keep reading letters until the denier finally agrees to do so. Once the denier says yes, there's no need to read the remaining letters. (You can turn the unread letters over to the denier afterward to read privately.)

Offer an immediate solution

Unfortunately, you can't leave it in the denier's hands to seek help. It's easy for deniers to make false promises about getting help that are all too easy to renege on as days pass.

Once the denier has agreed to do something about his or her LIB, you need to present the most viable solution immediately. If you have every necessary step laid out and ready to implement, you'll be able to steer the denier in the right direction without a moment of delay. Your preparedness removes any last excuse the denier may have, especially the excuse of not knowing what the first move should be.

Giving the denier this book might be a logical next step to try—after all, reading it worked for you. You could not only ask the denier to read this book but also volunteer to be in the denier's circle of trust and make a date to discuss the book afterward to make sure the denier used all the steps. However, you also need to investigate whether the denier's LIB is something that should be treated by an expert or an organization.

For example, using LIBs from the ADAPT list:

- *Abuse:* I've known families who asked their loved one who was in denial about being abused to agree to enter a shelter and get professional assistance in exiting the abusive situation.

- *Disorders:* For the person in denial about a psychological issue, the next step could be seeing a therapist later that day—an appointment you've scheduled ahead of time—then having the denier agree to undergo the treatments necessary to evaluate his or her LIB.

- *Addiction:* The arrangement with the addicts I've worked with is always to agree to enter a treatment center, see a therapist that day, and join an organization that may be able to treat their disease.

- *Physical issues:* For people in denial about a health issue, I've known people who set up a doctor's appointment for two hours after the sit-down so that the denier could immediately be driven to it. Afterward, they made the denier agree to a specific schedule for seeking medical advice on a more regular basis.

- *The Truth:* Someone in denial about mishandling money and sliding into serious debt might be asked to agree to keep an appointment that very day with a financial adviser or the bank they're in trouble with.

Sometimes there are several possible solutions you could offer the denier. By presenting the denier with various options, you'll have alternatives if he or she balks at your strongest suggestion. For example, instead of going to an inpatient treatment center, the denier may be more open to going to an outpatient center or visiting a therapist. That's why it's important to do a little homework prior to your sit-down to see what types of programs, doctors, and experts are available that are specifically focused on your denier's LIB. Whatever options you come up with, they should meet the following three criteria to be the most effective:

1. The proposed treatment is easy to access but difficult to leave. Choosing a treatment facility that's the best in the world may be a plus, but not if it's too expensive—or simply impossible—for the denier to get there. To ensure that the denier gets help, start by picking local options. However, if they suffer from a severe LIB, then find a place that is easy to get to but far enough from the denier's home that it's not as easy to leave. The further away the help is that you're proposing, the more likely the denier will stay there and receive the treatment they need.

2. The proposed treatment is easy to confirm. The solution you propose should be one that you—or any other person involved with the sit-down—can easily check in on to make sure the denier is going through with it. That can mean several things:

You could choose an expert who's willing to reveal how often the denier comes for treatment.

You could have the denier give you permission to check with the party providing treatment.

You could volunteer to take the denier to all treatments so that time and effort can never be the denier's excuse for not going.

3. The proposed treatment can be started ASAP. Time is of the essence once the wall of denial is finally down. Giving the denier any options that take even a few days to try doesn't work—the help needs to start right at that moment to achieve the best results. If not, it's possible for the denier to leave the sit-down and proceed to rebuild the wall even higher than it was before. Keeping a previously arranged appointment with an expert or specialist immediately after the sit-down is an option in some of the examples I just gave you, but again, the immediate action taken could be getting the denier to start using the principles in this book.

Prepare to make a sacrifice

Finally, if the denier refuses to get help despite the efforts made by everyone at the sit-down, you need to take a stand. Let the denier know that you respect that decision, but that you also can no longer stand by and watch what the denier is doing with his or her life. You have to be willing to do something that will make the denier rethink the decision to turn down your help. Depending on the LIB involved, you could take one or more of these actions:

- Vowing to end your friendship with the denier

- Calling the denier on his or her actions in front of others, regardless of who is present

- If the denier's LIB involves illegal activities, reporting those activities to local authorities

- Warning that you will no longer keep the denier's LIB a secret and will speak openly about it to others

Regardless of what you choose to do, you must draw some sort of line in the sand that the denier is aware you will cross if he or she doesn't seek immediate help.

18

What to Do When the Bricks Won't Break

Sometimes it's impossible to solve your LIB on your own.

Using the tools in this book, most people will discover their own denial, discover and put an end to their LIB, then rebalance their lives to keep their LIB in check for good. But I recognize that sometimes you simply can't take that journey alone, even with all the support in the world from your family, friends, and others in your circle of trust. There are certain LIBs that, no matter how hard you try, are extremely difficult to break free of. Some walls of denial are too high to see over, and too thick to tear down, by yourself.

If this is your situation, the first thing I want you to realize—no, I need you to realize—is that you're far from alone. Many people who read this book will not be able to break through their own wall of denial. Many people just like you need some sort of outside resource to help them thoroughly address their denial. There are millions of people in the world right now—some with your LIB, others with their own unique LIB—who are in your same exact situation.

The second thing I need you to realize is that you're not in any way weaker than those people who have been able to break their

BE PREPARED TO COMMIT TO
AT LEAST SIX MONTHS OF HELP

At this point, you know what LIB you're in denial about, but the fact that you have a LIB that defies the tools in this book makes one thing perfectly clear to me: your denial runs so deep that you're going to need to spend time with a professional who treats your LIB to finally erase it from your life.

As much as I wish I could promise that your LIB will disappear after one or two visits with a specialist like the ones recommended by the organizations in the Recommended Resources, it's simply not going to be that easy. That's why you need to accept your denial and promise me—no, promise yourself—that you'll commit to spending a minimum of six months in treatment.

Is it possible to beat your LIB sooner than that? Yes, sometimes it is. If you have an addiction, you can seek out a thirty- to ninety-day inpatient treatment center that specializes in your LIB. These types of centers allow deniers to experience a lot more recovery treatment in a shorter period of time. But if no such facility is available and you find that you need to get help on an outpatient basis, understand that the process will be slower and your results will take longer than thirty to ninety days.

If your LIB isn't addiction-related, I recommend that you look within your own community for a therapist or psychiatrist who specializes in your condition and commit to treatment from that specialist for at least six months.

If you find a professional with a specialty in what you're going through, the six months of treatment I'm recommending will change your life forever.

own denial and take control of their LIB using this book. In fact, recognizing that you can't beat your LIB already makes you stronger because you can admit it. I want to congratulate you because, by admitting that fact, you've opened up a door that will bring your life in balance. Just because you can't open up that door all the way yet doesn't mean you've failed. If you've tried everything in this book and still haven't succeeded, then I want you to take pride in yourself for three reasons:

1. You tried—and you're a winner for that reason alone.

2. You acknowledge that you're in denial and have a LIB, which is a lot more than many people in the world allow themselves to see.

3. You understand that you need a little more help, and admitting that takes an enormous amount of strength and self-honesty.

If you need any further proof that you can still turn your life around, then the best example I can give you is myself. I know what it's like to be right where you are now because that was my situation. I couldn't beat my alcoholism by myself. I couldn't beat my many drug addictions on my own. I couldn't tackle certain other LIBs that crept into my life without the help of others. It took professional help to break down my denial, and because that happened, I'm now not just in the happiest place I've ever been in my life but able to help others find that place as well.

You've now opened up your eyes to the gravity of your situation and fully understand that you have a LIB that is greater than yourself, but it's still an issue that you're capable of conquering—even if I may not be the one who guides you through the entire process. If you've exhausted every option in this book and utilized every tool, then there are some other effective forms of support I can recommend that will give you the additional help you need.

The first place you can turn to is my recovery network (www .interventionnetwork.ning.com), which provides information and resources on a wide variety of addictions. If you can't find what you're looking for there, the Recommended Resources section that follows lists some of the top organizations that I recommend for getting more information about your LIB, finding a credible specialist to treat it, and even locating a support group in your area so you can see that you're not alone. Such organizations have helped millions of deniers—as I said, several of them were responsible for helping me with my own LIBs. You and I have found your LIB over the past few chapters, but if it's too strong for us to beat using this book, then please let one of the organizations listed in the following section put you in touch with a specialist who can finish the job we've started together.

Recommended Resources

ABUSE

Child Abuse
Childhelp (childhelp.org): This nonprofit organization assists with the physical, emotional, educational, and spiritual needs of abused, neglected, and at-risk children. It also runs an anonymous service hotline (800-4-A-CHILD) that offers crisis intervention, information, literature, and referrals to thousands of emergency, social service, and support resources.

Domestic Violence
National Domestic Violence Hotline (ndvh.org): NDVH is a nonprofit organization that provides crisis intervention, information, and referral to victims of domestic violence, perpetrators, friends, and families. Its twenty-four-hour toll-free number (800-799-SAFE or 800-787-3224) is the only domestic violence hotline in the nation with access to more than five thousand shelters and domestic violence programs across the United States, Puerto Rico, and the U.S. Virgin Islands.

Elder Abuse

National Center on Elder Abuse (ncea.aoa.gov): This program of the U.S. Administration on Aging acts as a national resource center dedicated to the prevention of elder mistreatment. NCEA also runs a national elder-care locator (800-677-1116), Monday to Friday, 9:00 a.m.–8:00 p.m. Eastern (except on national holidays).

Pet Abuse

Humane Society of the United States (hsus.org): HSUS is the largest and most effective animal protection organization in the United States. It offers advice on what to do if you see animal abuse, how to find your nearest animal control agency, and information on locating a shelter in your area.

Sexual Abuse (General)

Rape, Abuse, and Incest National Network (rainn.org): RAINN is the nation's largest anti–sexual assault organization. Its nationwide partnership of more than 1,100 rape treatment hotlines provides victims of sexual assault with free, confidential services around the clock through the National Sexual Assault Hotline (800-656-HOPE) and the National Sexual Assault Online Hotline, located at the RAINN Web site.

Sexual Abuse (Men)

Male Survivor (malesurvivor.org): This organization provides resources and support for men who were sexually victimized as children, adolescents, or adults. It also has a resource directory that helps individuals find a professional therapist in their area.

DISORDERS (PSYCHOLOGICAL AND EMOTIONAL)

General Mental Health Issues

Substance Abuse and Mental Health Services Administration, National Mental Health Information Center (mentalhealth.samhsa .gov): SAMHSA provides information about nearly every type of mental health issue, either through its Web site or over its toll-free hotline (800-662-HELP). It can also help you locate a treatment facility in your area. For more information, see the SAMHSA entry under "Substance Abuse."

Mental Health America (nmha.org): Mental Health America (formerly known as the National Mental Health Association) is the leading nonprofit organization in the United States specializing in mental health—it has 320 affiliates nationwide. Search its Web site or call the hotline (800-969-6642), and you'll be put on the fast track for finding information, support groups, treatment centers, and organizations on nearly every type of mental health disorder.

National Alliance on Mental Illness (nami.org): NAMI is the nation's largest grassroots organization for people with mental illness and their families; it has affiliates in every state and in more than 1,100 communities throughout the United States. Its helpline (800-950-6264) offers general information on most illnesses, referrals, and support.

ADHD

Children and Adults with Attention Deficit Hyperactivity Disorder (chadd.org): With over 16,000 members in 200 chapters throughout the United States, CHADD is the nation's leading nonprofit organization specializing in ADHD. It provides education, advocacy, and support for both individuals with ADHD and their families, either through its Web site or over its toll-free hotline (800-233-4050).

Anxiety Disorders

Anxiety Disorders Association of America (adaa.org): ADAA is a national nonprofit organization dedicated to the prevention, treatment, and cure of anxiety disorders. It provides information and therapist recommendations to help treat general anxiety, OCD, PTSD, panic disorders, social anxiety, and phobias.

Bipolar Disorder and Depression

Depression and Bipolar Support Alliance (ndmda.org): DBSA is a leading, patient-directed, national organization that provides hope, help, and support to those living with depression or bipolar disorder. It reaches nearly 5 million people through its educational materials and programs, exhibit materials, and media activities and offers more than 1,000 peer-run support groups.

Obsessive-Compulsive Disorders

Obsessive-Compulsive Foundation (ocfoundation.org): One of the best organizations focused on organizing and promoting OCD-related support groups and OCF affiliates throughout the world, this international not-for-profit foundation also offers a wide assortment of literature and referral services for professionals who specialize in treating the disorder.

Post-Traumatic Stress Disorder

National Center for PTSD (ncptsd.va.gov): NCPTSD is the world's leading research and educational center on PTSD. Its ultimate purpose is to improve the well-being and status of American veterans through research, education, and training in the science, diagnosis, and treatment of PTSD and other stress-related disorders.

Postpartum Depression

Postpartum Support International (postpartum.net): This organization's mission is to increase awareness about the emotional changes women experience during and after pregnancy. It also runs a hotline (800-944-4773) that can refer you to the appropriate resources, including emergency services, in your area.

ADDICTIONS

General Addiction Issues

Intervention and Recovery Network (interventionnetwork.ning .com): The Intervention and Recovery Network is a community for those in recovery and a resource for those people seeking information, understanding, and help for themselves or their loved ones suffering from addiction. The community supports its members through chats and forums and shares experiences by posting via blog or video.

Alcoholism

Alcoholics Anonymous (aa.org): Alcoholics Anonymous is an informal group of men and women who meet to share their experiences to help others recover from alcoholism. There are no dues or fees to join. Today AA is found in over 180 countries and has over 113,000 groups and more than 2 million members worldwide.

Eating Disorders

National Eating Disorders Association (nationaleatingdisorders .org): NEDA is a nonprofit organization that supports individuals and families affected by eating disorders. Its toll-free helpline (800-931-2237) provides information and offers referrals for various recovery options, including treatment professionals and prevention volunteers.

Nicotine Addiction

Smokefree.gov: Created by the Tobacco Control Research Branch of the National Cancer Institute, this Web site lets you decide on the type of help that best fits your needs. You can choose the online step-by-step cessation guide or the local, state, and national quit-lines (800-QUITNOW).

Problem Gambling

National Council on Problem Gambling (ncpgambling.org): This organization is the national advocate for programs and services that assist problem gamblers and their families. It also runs the National Problem Gambling Helpline Network (800-522-4700), a national hotline that helps locate resources in your area.

Sexual Compulsion

Society for the Advancement of Sexual Health (sash.net): The nonprofit organization SASH is the only association dedicated to helping individuals who suffer from out-of-control sexual behavior. It provides up-to-date research, information, education, and other resources about sexual addiction, as well as a directory to help you find a therapeutic professional, medical institution, or treatment facility.

Substance Abuse

Substance Abuse and Mental Health Services Administration (samhsa.gov): A division of the Department of Health and Human Services, SAMHSA runs three centers for the treatment and prevention of substance abuse, as well as for mental health services. It offers help with finding nearby treatment services through its twenty-four-hour helpline (800-662-4357), and its National Clearinghouse for Alcohol and Drug Information (NCADI) provides information about substance abuse prevention, intervention, and treatment policies, programs, and practices (ncadi.samhsa.gov).

PHYSICAL (HEALTH) ISSUES

General Health Issues
Centers for Disease Control and Prevention (cdc.gov): The CDC provides facts, resources, statistics, and treatment options for nearly every possible health-related issue.

Allergies
American Academy of Allergy, Asthma, and Immunology (aaaai .org): The AAAAI is the largest professional medical organization in the United States devoted to allergy and immunology diseases—it has close to 6,500 members in the United States, Canada, and sixty other countries. The AAAAI represents asthma specialists, clinical immunologists, allied health professionals, and others with a special interest in the research and treatment of allergic disease.

Birth Defects and Other Pregnancy-Related Health Issues
March of Dimes (marchofdimes.com): Dedicated to improving the health of babies by preventing birth defects, premature birth, and infant mortality, the March of Dimes provides information and resources on all types of birth defects, genetic conditions, and the obstacles and infections that some pregnant women may experience and be in denial about, including anemia, hyperthyroidism, amniotic fluid complications, listeriosis, and miscarriage.

Birth Defects and Developmental Disabilities
National Center on Birth Defects and Developmental Disabilities (cdc.gov/ncbddd/): The NCBDDD provides information and resources on a wide range of health issues that affect babies, children, and adults, including fetal alcohol syndrome, autism, intellectual disabilities, vision impairment, cerebral palsy, and blood disorders.

Cancer

American Cancer Society (cancer.org): The ACS is a nationwide, community-based, voluntary health organization with more than 3,400 local offices. It provides up-to-date information on all aspects of cancer through a toll-free information line (800-ACS-2345), its Web site, and published materials.

Cardiovascular Disease

American Heart Association (americanheart.org): The ADA is a national nonprofit health agency that specializes in cardiovascular disease. Its Web site and toll-free hotline (800-AHA-USA-1) offer information on finding a local office, risk assessments, and treatment options, as well as other helpful resources on all areas of heart health, including arrhythmia, high cholesterol, heart attacks, high blood pressure, and peripheral artery disease (PAD). It also runs the American Stroke Association, which concentrates on the care, research, and prevention of strokes (888-4-STROKE).

Communication Disorders

National Institute on Deafness and Other Communication Disorders (nidcd.nih.gov): Part of the U.S. Department of Health and Human Services, the NIDCD's main job is supporting biomedical research to help prevent, detect, diagnose, and treat communication disorders. Its extensive directory lists selected national organizations that provide information on hearing and deafness, balance, smell and taste, voice, and speech and language disorders.

Dermatological Issues

American Academy of Dermatology (aad.org): With a membership of over 16,000, the ADA represents virtually all practicing dermatologists in the United States. The organization can help find a doctor in your area, through either its Web site or its hotline (888-462-DERM), assist you in locating a skin cancer screening center, and provide information on diagnosing and treating a variety of skin conditions, from acne to xeroderma pigmentosum.

Diabetes

American Diabetes Association (diabetes.org): Conducting programs in all fifty states, the ADA is the nation's leading nonprofit health organization. Dedicated to diabetes research, information, and advocacy, the ADA's mission is to prevent and cure diabetes, as well as improve the lives of all people affected by the disease.

Eye or Vision Problems

American Optometric Association (aoa.org): The AOA is the premier authority in the optometric profession and can help you find an optometrist in your area. With more than 35,000 members in 6,500 U.S. communities, the AOA provides information on symptoms and treatment options for every type of eye and vision problem, including astigmatism, cataracts, eye coordination issues, glaucoma, macular degeneration, presbyopia, and retinitis pigmentosa.

Hair Loss

American Hair Loss Association (americanhairloss.org): The AHLA is the only national nonprofit membership organization dedicated to educating those affected by the emotionally devastating disease of hair loss (alopecia) and improving their lives. It provides information on treatment options for every type of alopecia, which affects both men and women.

STIs

American Social Health Association (ashastd.org): ASHA is a trusted nonprofit organization that offers access to in-depth information about sexually transmitted infections (STIs), including resources, referrals, and support groups. Its STI Resource Center Hotline (800-227-8922) also has on-staff health communication specialists available to answer STI questions on such topics as transmission, risk reduction, prevention, testing, and treatment.

(THE) TRUTH

General Personality Issues

American Psychological Association (apa.org): The APA is the largest association of psychologists worldwide, representing over 148,000 practitioners. A few clicks on its Web site or a quick call to its hotline (800-964-2000) can get you a referral to a psychologist in your area.

The Death of a Child

The Compassionate Friends (compassionatefriends.org): TCF is a national nonprofit organization that offers support to families grieving over the death of a child of any age and from any cause. The group has about six hundred meeting locations throughout the United States; to find one in your area, call the hotline (877-969-0010).

The Death of a Family Member (for Children)

Fernside (fernside.org): Fernside is a nonprofit organization that offers support and advocacy to grieving families, particularly children, who have experienced a death. They provide—free of charge—peer support groups, summer camp and retreat experiences, and in-school grief groups, education, and training.

Emotional Issues

Emotions Anonymous (emotions.anonymous.org): This organization sets up weekly meetings for individuals trying to recover from an emotional dilemma such as anger, grief, anxiety, low self-esteem, abnormal fears, resentment, jealousy, guilt, despair, fatigue, tension, boredom, loneliness, withdrawal, negative thinking, worry, or compulsive behavior.

Financial Debt

Debtors Anonymous (debtorsanonymous.org): This nonprofit fellowship holds over five hundred meetings throughout the United States and uses a twelve-step program to help members share their experiences about debt.

Relationship Issues

American Association for Marriage and Family Therapy (therapist locator.net): Representing over 24,000 marriage and family therapists throughout the United States and Canada and overseas, AAMFT is the premier association in the field of marriage and family therapy. Its Web site can help you find a local therapist who can handle a variety of marital problems, and it provides information on a wide range of other physical and psychological disorders, from Alzheimer's disease to suicide.

Acknowledgments

This book has been an amazing experience for me.

To be able to help people in need and stop the suffering they may have in some part of their life. To give them not just hope but possibly freedom from anything that may be holding them back. But none of it would have happened without so many people coming together, joining forces, and wanting to get this message out there.

First, I'd like to thank Kary McHoul, who introduced me to Lisa Sharkey at HarperCollins to get this process moving, and all the people there who took a leap of faith with me on this: again, Lisa Sharkey, Claudia Boutote, Mark Tauber, Terri Leonard, Lisa Zuniga, Laura Ingman, Jan Baumer, Gideon Weil, and the entire HarperOne team.

Of course, this would not have been possible at all if I didn't have the best writing partner there is: Myatt Murphy. To take my many thoughts and put them on paper so you can understand them all is nothing short of genius, and his background in psychology really helped bring out the clinical component of this book. I also want to thank Greg Suess at ROAR who represented us though this process.

I have to thank all of the people that, in one way or another, have touched me and given me the understanding and education that's allowed this book to happen: Ed Storti, Dr. Jim deJarnette, the professionals at the Betty Ford Center, Joel Osteen, Christopher Kennedy Lawford, Oprah Winfrey, Dr. Drew Pinsky, Jane Velez-Mitchell, Nancy Grace, Larry King, AJ Hammer, Brooke Anderson, Robin McGraw, Brad Lamm, Rosie O'Donnell, Howard Bergman, Dr. Laura Berman, Bob Greene, Rory Freedman, Kim Barnouin, Rick Warren, Eckhart Tolle, Zhi Gang Sha, Randy Pausch, Jeffrey Zaslow, Mark Hyman, Rhonda Byrne, Larry Winget, Suzanne Somers, Ardice Farrow, Mark Smith, and Chris Spencer.

I want to thank the amazing team that I work with, and have worked with in the past, at Intervention911. You all made it possible for me to find the time to get this book done.

I also want to thank those who believed in me (and continue to believe in me) on the A&E hit show *Intervention:* Sam Mettler, Dan Partland, Colleen Conaway, Gina Nocero, Gary Benz, Karen Pinto, Jeff Weaver, the entire crew past and present at GRB, and my fellow colleagues Jeff VanVonderen, Candy Finnigan, and Tara Fields.

I especially want to thank my friends and family, who had to tolerate my dysfunctional behavior while I was battling my own denial: Eric McLaughlin; Mom; Dad; my sister's family, the Shoemakers; all of my aunts, uncles, and cousins; as well as my extended family and friends, especially Andrea Diener—a dear friend whose life was shorted as a result of her ex-husband's addiction—and my Uncle Jack (who we lost way too early).

And, the best for last, thank you, God. Without my spirituality, none of this would have been possible.